From Pulpit to Purpose

Pulpit Education—Training Leaders for Impact in the Black Church

Dewayne Tapscott

CYPRESS

Copyright © 2025 by Dewayne Tapscott

Cataloging-in-Publication Data

Tapscott, Dewayne (Brice Dewayne), 1972-

From pulpit to purpose: pulpit education—training leaders for impact in the Black church/ Dewayne Tapscott.

p. cm.

ISBN: 979-8-89733-017-1 (pbk.); 979-8-89733-018-8 (ebook)

1. Preaching. 2. Black churches. 3. Pastoral theology. I. Author. II. Title.

253.08996073—dc20

Cover design by Brad McKinnon and Brittany Vander Maas.

For information:

Cypress Publications
3625 Helton Drive
PO Box HCU
Florence, AL 35630

www.hcu.edu

I wholeheartedly dedicate this book to my late mother, Ruthie Nell Tapscott; my father, Arbie Tapscott; my brother, Laymon Moore; and my sister, Cornelious "Nita" Draper. They all instilled in me the value of a strong work ethic. From that foundational lesson, I have grown, and through my own first-hand experiences, I teach my congregation that we are the sum total of what others invest into our lives. I am forever grateful for their initial investment, which has helped shape me into the man I am today.

Acknowledgments

I give all thanks to God for guiding me through this project, *From Pulpit To Purpose*.

Special thanks to my wife, Tera, for your unwavering support.

To my children, Skylar, Kyle, Brianne, and Bricen, I pray God continues to bless your lives.

To my granddaughter Brielle, Pop-Pop loves you.

Thank you to my brother, Danny Tapscott, for your continual support and encouragement.

To Southwest Church of Christ (Huntsville, Alabama) and Piney Grove Church of Christ (Winfield, Alabama), thank you for allowing me to serve as your minister.

Lastly, to Sherron Fantroy, I appreciate your editorial assistance on this project.

Be Blessed
Dr. Dewayne Tapscott

Contents

Preface

This book provides ministers, educators, and church leaders with key principles and insights for effective pulpit ministry, focusing on mentorship, study, and life transformation through God's Word.

Enhancing the Youth in the Local Black Churches

A significant decline has been brewing within the local Black church community for quite some time. This decline largely stems from a lack of Christian training and spiritual guidance for young Black teenagers. As a result, many churches are experiencing an exodus of youth. Peter Paris pens in his book *The Social Teaching Of The Black Churches*, "The Black Christian Church has been the lifeline of the Black community" (1985, 25). Without these vibrant churches in the local community, our homes and neighborhoods would be in much worse shape than they appear today. Many Black children do not come from traditional families. Instead, they are raised in broken homes, often due to divorce, or by single parents and relatives. Because of these circumstances, many young people turn to the streets and gangs for guidance, love, and sometimes even protection.

To make a meaningful impact on society, each local congregation needs to do some "deep soul searching" among themselves. Jeremiah writes, *"The harvest is past, the summer is ended, and we are not saved"* (Jer 8:20 ESV). What educational and spiritual strategies does the local church need to prepare the next generation for the ongoing struggle for greater freedom and wholeness? When leaders of the Black church neglect to analyze and address the suffering within their communities, they hinder their ministry's ability to be a true beacon of Christ's light. William Barclay in *The Black Church* writes, "Christianity was never meant to withdraw a man from life; it was meant to equip him for better life" (2010, 47). If the church fails the community, the youth will drift away because they don't see the relevance of the church in their lives.

After speaking with over one hundred ministers in the local Black churches across various states, a common concern emerges: How do we effectively equip our young Black future leaders with resilience to survive and thrive? These preachers respond that most Black churches rarely have a dedicated youth minister, especially in smaller cities. When leadership cannot relate to or connect with their youth, they face an uphill battle. The pandemic further exposed this disconnect, as many Black churches lost vital connections with their young people due to the absence of social media and online ministry platforms.

Effective youth ministry leadership requires dedicated preparation and strong support. Unfortunately, many young black ministry leaders experience burnout early due to a lack of support and proper training. Church leaders must commit themselves to educating and compensating our young leaders for the future. Regrettably, many congregations have yet to prioritize spiritual education for their youth ministers.

The power of positive words can transform communities, states, and even entire nations. Yet, as Dr. Ted W.

Engstrom and Dr. Ron Jenson state in *The Making Of A Mentor*, most young people have never reached half of their potential because no one has believed in them (2005, 17).

To capture the youth in the local Black church, the congregation's leaders must think outside the box. We must bridge the gap between traditional youth ministry and the high-tech world our young people live in. We cannot succeed as isolated individuals. Instead, we must work together, functioning as one body in Christ, to raise the next generation of leaders.

Our prayer should be to stop dreaming about the vision of a thriving youth ministry and instead take action to groom those leaders today. The declining lifeline in the Black church must be revived. Leaders must learn how to reach the youth where they are, whether that's the neighborhood basketball courts, football practice fields, baseball facilities, or high school track and field events. Authors Anne Wimberly, Sandra Barnes, and Karma Johnson provide practical insights in *Youth Ministry In The Black Church*. They emphasize that the greatest challenge facing our churches today is the availability and accessibility of youth and their families (2013, 87). If there is ever a time for the local Black church to be on the move for God, then the time is now, so that we can prepare our future leaders for tomorrow.

- ** The following chapters will be geared towards *From Pulpit To Purpose!* **
- Training Leaders for Impact in the Black Church!

* * *

Discussion Questions

How can we enhance our Black Youth in ministry?

Will our Black youth remain "Relevant" or become "Irrelevant" in the twenty-first century?

How can we connect a disconnected generation? There is a noticeable disconnect between the elders (leadership) of the Black church and the youth of today. Dale Andrews, in *Practical Theology For Black Churches*, raises the question: Why do some young Black youth feel as if they are disjoined from the church?" (2002, 88ff)

Jesus ministered to many, but He focused on a few (Matt 22:14). As mentors for our young Black ministers, can you name five "mentees" who show great potential for the future of the Lord's church?

What does the statement "Do not discourage your mentee by your silence" mean? Name some reasons why many local churches have failed to groom and train our youth for leadership roles, such as future elders, deacons, and ministers. J. Herbert Hinkle in *Soul Winning In Black Churches* highlights that many Black congregations have lost the traditional study habits of soul-winning, leading to internal crises within the church (Mark 16:15–16). During a group youth study, ask each young person to explain what it means to be saved and how to teach the plan of salvation to someone who is lost. The church's primary focus must be soul-winning for Jesus Christ (1973, 45ff).

What practical steps can local congregations take to involve community youth and encourage their active participation? Examples include youth feeding programs, youth lectures, vocal camp workshops, and the often-overlooked "Black Lads To Leaders" program.

How is the role of the Black church declining in the

lives of our youth? How strong is leadership in training and educating the youth? What positive steps can the church and individual Christians take to reverse this trend and better serve our young people?

* * *

This introduction is a revised chapter in *In Christ's Image: A Guide to Youth and Family Ministry*. Edited by W. Kirk Brothers. Heritage Christian Leadership Institute Series. Florence, AL: Heritage Christian University Press, 2024.

Chapter 1
Mentoring Preachers in the Local Churches

MANY INDIVIDUALS DO NOT HAVE the luxury of time or financial resources to pursue seminary education. This book aims to equip deacons, elders, Sunday School teachers, ministerial interns, and ministers of the gospel to better prepare themselves in lesson planning and delivery. The pulpit is serious business because it is centered on God's divine work—His spiritual mission. The potential to do harm to the minds and lives of others should prompt us to think, pray, study, and examine the Word of God thoroughly before stepping into the pulpit.

The apostle Paul reminds his young protégé Timothy in (2 Tim 4:2 ESV) *"Be ready in season and out of season; reprove, rebuke, and exhort, with complete patience and teaching."* To be an effective preacher, one must understand how to build spiritually and practically. Jesus spoke about building in the gospel of Luke *"For which of you, desiring to build a tower, does not first sit down and count the cost, whether he has enough to complete it?"* (Luke 14:28). God assists the builder of sermons. It is through daily communion with God that our preaching style becomes effective. Jesus also spoke

about feeding his sheep in *"He said to him the third time,
"Simon, son of John, do you love me?" Peter was grieved because he
said to him the third time, "Do you love me?" and he said to him,
"Lord, you know everything; you know that I love you." Jesus said
to him, "Feed my sheep"* (John 21:17).

Harold T. Bryson and James C. Taylor, in their book
Building Sermons to Meet People's Needs, state: "You have to
prepare yourself for communication with the people.
Therefore, you have to write for the ear and not the eye"
(1980, 89). The core purpose of preaching is to proclaim
the good news about Jesus Christ to the unconverted while
teaching the foundational principles of the Gospel.

Prepare your sermons as if you are preaching before a
community of preachers and a community of saints. Many
preachers often wonder, "Where do I begin when invited
to preach at another church?" Clifton Guthrie in *From Pew
to Pulpit* quotes Karl Barth: "To have to speak from a
particular text to a particular congregation in an actual
situation is in itself a dangerous undertaking" (2005, 22).
When preparing a lesson, it is wise to choose a good Bible
translation. As you craft your message, keep in mind the
Five W's:

1. Who (who wrote it),
2. What (what does it say about God),
3. When (timeline),
4. Where (can I trace the journey),
5. Why (why should I pay attention).

Working ahead by a few weeks is beneficial so that
you're not constantly rushing. Be cautious with topical
sermons. They can go off track if the preacher seeks scriptural "proof" for a preconceived idea. Expository sermons

can also falter if they uncover obscure meanings in a passage that lacks clarity and a relevant application that relates to the congregation.

Before Preaching the Text—Know the Text

When preparing your sermons for your audience, it is essential to preach sermons that are meaningful to you. If your sermon does not resonate with you personally, it will likely not resonate with your listeners either. Calvin Miller once noted, "The Church needs to know what the world wants to hear and yet also find a way to give what it needs to hear in a sermon" (2001, 14).

The church would be lost without preachers who possess the ability to engage in advanced study of Scripture. To truly understand any biblical text, one should begin with prayer. Every preacher needs a method for studying, understanding, and teaching the Scriptures. Your method should include, but not be limited to:

- Identifying the text and its genre;
- Discerning the main point of the story or passage;
- Understanding the context (is it literal, canonical, historical, cultural, or geographical).

Be sure to gather all available study aids, such as commentaries and lexicons, that will assist you, especially with the original translation. This is crucial because a word left out or misunderstood can significantly alter the meaning of the entire passage. Language in our culture today is changing quickly, making careful study even more important. Solomon writes in Proverbs 22:6, the question that parents often ask is, 'How do I train my child according to his way?' Since every child is different, our approach must be tailored to each individual's way of learning. As Allan Mosley states in *From the Study to the Pulpit,* "Our souls must be prepared to preach" (2017, 49).

Variety of Sermons

- Deductive Sermon: Begins with the main idea and develops it through two or three supporting points, ending with application and conclusion.
- Inductive Sermon: The main idea may only become clear toward the end of the sermon, guiding listeners through the process of discovery.
- Exegesis: Means "to lead or interpret" and involves understanding the background of the text, including cultural, historical, and contextual factors.
- Topical Sermons: In the book titled *Preaching with Conviction,* author Kenton Anderson quotes a line from Robert Capon, "Topical sermons are like topical anesthetics. They don't go deep" (2001, 65). The Bible does not build on human experience but rather rearranges and transforms it.

Crafting Your Message

Every preacher I have listened to displays a unique study pattern. Dr. Tony V. Lewis highlights in *The Message and the Messenger* the importance of practical study methods, such as the A.E.I.O.U. Bible study approach (2014, 47–48):

- **A** = Ask questions.
- **E** = Emphasize the words (Say the sentence a number of times, emphasizing different words each time you read it).
- **I** = Investigate (Look for the answer to one or more of your questions).
- **O** = Other scriptures (Read some cross references as well as other scriptures about this subject).
- **U** = Use it (How can you apply this verse in your life?)

Always write in the language of the ear. Speak your sermon aloud while writing it to make it come alive. Engage your audience from the start by creating interest in your message.

What is biblical preaching? It is simply staying rooted in the Bible! The Word of God is central to our tradition, our heritage, and our culture. A genuine desire to know Scripture is vital. James W. Cox, in *A Guide to Biblical Preaching*, expresses that "the purpose of a scriptural text is a reminder who we are, where we are going, and what we ought to be doing" (1976, 44). Many people today are not interested in what went on centuries ago. They want to know how to live now. Unless an individual first hears the gospel of Christ themselves, they will be unprepared to proclaim the Word of God to others.

Avoiding the Pitfalls of Distorted Theology

Personal devotion is essential not only for your growth but also for the good of others. Distorted theology, poor teaching, and ineffective ministry often stem from not rightly dividing the Word of God. A man's devotion directly influences his success in life and relationships.

The Lord gave Joshua good instructions as it was penned in "*This Book of the Law shall not depart from your mouth, but you shall meditate on it day and night, so that you may be careful to do according to all that is written in it. For then you will make your way prosperous, and then you will have good success*" (Josh 1:8). By regularly spending time in God's Word, we too can be successful Christians and faithful ministers, just as Joshua was. Daily meditation should be the day-in and day-out lifestyle of God's people. It is in our reflective thought process that we see answered prayers and avoid certain pitfalls.

When we begin our daily devotions, consistency is the key, even if the time we spend is brief. We can always increase the duration as we grow in discipline. It would be wise counsel for you to find an accountability partner, someone you trust, to encourage and remind you to remain faithful in your devotion time with God.

The call of God is real. Are you following and obeying His instructions? We live in an ungodly culture, and as preachers (and believers), we have the responsibility to set the tone in the world, in every community, and in our respective neighborhoods. In order to set the godly example, we must be the best that we can be. Everyone has a role in ministry, but not everyone fulfills their ministerial duties fully. Our responsibilities include

- teaching sound doctrine,
- mentoring older men,
- guiding older women, and
- teaching the younger men and women the ways of the Lord.

The work of God is a splendid calling. Therefore, it's crucial to learn how to step back from negative influences and things that do not align with the Word of God. An older mentor once taught me that about "The Power of Delete (the importance of discarding negativity)." You don't have to listen to every critical word or accept every negative speech. When you encounter people who don't want to see you succeed, see you do well in life, or support you when times are tough—it's time to press the delete button. A vivid illustration comes to mind: when you type something on your computer that you want to remove, you can hit Ctrl Z, which deletes what you just typed. The danger of not deleting certain negative influences is that our brains often convince us that what is done cannot be undone, making us believe those words or actions are final.

Wise Advice: You don't need everybody in your chapter of life, which is also known as your book of your life. You're in control of writing your destiny, so guard yourself of the negativity and dangerous gossip that pollutes your mind and spirit. To make a lasting spiritual impact, remember that we serve a maximum God. When your priorities are out of balance, you will never advance in life or in your ministry. When your priorities are not right with God, excuses will multiply, and you will miss out on His abundant blessings.

Chapter 2
What Is Pulpit Education?

PULPIT EDUCATION IS the process of learning the essential protocols for studying the Word of God while effectively delivering it to your audience. God has a plan for our lives, and we should strive to excel in fulfilling it to the highest degree. The pulpit was never designed for a person to simply share their favorite story, recount a recent camping excursion, or seek to embarrass someone with whom they're not in agreement. Instead, it was created to make a profound impact on those we encounter. Matthew writes, *"You are the salt of the earth, but if salt has lost its taste, how shall its saltiness be restored? It is no longer good for anything except to be thrown out and trampled under people's feet"* (Matt 5:13). To make an effective spiritual impact on the life of someone else, spiritual impact starts with your daily devotion and prayer. As Gwen Smith writes in *I Want It All*, "God's grace is greater than my attitude, pride, wounds, struggles, wandering way, limitations, and weakness" (2016, 37).

When approaching the pulpit, the primary goal should be to proclaim God's Word to a lost, hurting, and dying world. God spoke to Solomon, and Ezra echoes this in *"If my people who are called by my name humble themselves and pray and seek my face and turn from their wicked ways, then I will hear from heaven and will forgive their sin and heal their land"* (2 Chron 7:14). Ministry is not merely about completing a task; it's about demonstrating our love for God through prayer, unwavering commitment, and dedicated service.

Knowing the Value of Another Day in Ministry

There are many things to remember before quitting the ministry. Often, preachers find themselves physically exhausted, experiencing burnout, and contemplating a shift to a different occupation or vocation. Before making such a decision, there are two important truths to consider:

1. **Remember Whom You Work for:** Ministry has increasingly become a "market-driven vocation" for many preachers. However, we must never forget that we work for God! We don't work for the church, the community, or the elders; ultimately, our employer is God Himself. He will reward us according to our works. As John writes, *"Behold, I am coming soon, bringing my recompense with me, to repay each one for what he has done. I am the Alpha and the Omega, the first and the last, the beginning and the end"* (Rev 22:12). It's God's perspective on our service that truly matters.

2. **Remember Why You Go to Work:** You go to work because you are called by God, not by man, to preach the gospel. It's common to hear that ministry is a low-paying job, but the good

news is that your calling is a privileged opportunity. Never underestimate or overestimate your importance. Don't allow the actions of others who let you down to diminish your spirit. An older mentor once told me, "One reason we get knocked down in ministry is because we believe the best about people, and just when we need them the most, they end up letting us down." The author wrote *"looking to Jesus, the founder and perfecter of our faith, who for the joy that was set before him endured the cross, despising the shame, and is seated at the right hand of the throne of God"* in (Heb 12:2).

As we strive to be the best pulpiteers we can be, it's vital to S.O.A.K. ourselves in God's word to build our faith. No matter what challenges we face in life, the way we walk in faith reflects to the world the God we serve. There comes a time when we must stop "showcasing" our vulnerabilities and start "showcasing" Jesus. Paul writes, *"The Lord is at hand; do not be anxious about anything, but in everything by prayer and supplication with thanksgiving let your requests be made known to God. And the peace of God, which surpasses all understanding, will guard your hearts and your minds in Christ Jesus"* (Phil 4:6–7). Jan G. Linn, in his book *22 Keys to Being a Minister*, emphasizes: "Work your strengths, not your job. When what we do turns out to be something we truly enjoy, spiritual energy flows unhindered in all we do" (2003, 76). In essence, before you consider quitting, it's imperative that you recognize the value of another day. Every new day is an opportunity to serve God and impact lives.

Public Silence Turns into Public Watching

All of us should be about our Father's business in making disciples. The world has been watching us for years, listening to us talk the talk, but not always seeing us walk the walk. If a congregation isn't open to welcoming the lost into their midst, then they are not truly fulfilling their role as disciple makers. Any participation in life involves interactions with strangers. It's important to ask ourselves:

- How is the church doing in engaging with those unfamiliar to us today?
- How genuine is our hospitality toward visitors?

Hospitality demands transformation within us, as God's presence is often revealed through strangers.

We often sing a song in the black congregations, "I'm Glad to be in His Service One More Time," but there is a distinction between worship service and kingdom service. Worship service is about honoring God, remembering Him, worshiping Him, and being thankful of the sacrifice His Son made on the cross for our salvation. Kingdom service, however, means that I am spiritually alert for God's calling and that I am about My Father's business. Being about His business involves allowing the power of God to work in me and through me, always seeking new opportunities to share the gospel of Christ. It's about attempting great things for Him because every day is a new day in Him. Greg McIntosh, in his book *The 10 Key Roles of a Pastor*, emphasizes the importance of knowing your role as a minister (2021, 54–55):

- All ministers wear the speaker's hat: They are to preach the Word, know God, know themselves, and know the text. Communicate so people will remember.
- All ministers wear the coach's hat: Successful coaches recruit. Listed are a few recruiting suggestions;

a. Look at every person as a potential team member.
b. Encourage people to serve the Lord on the basis of their love for Him.
c. Don't downplay the role: Magnify it.
d. Don't recruit in the hallway. Rather, make appointments to sit down and discuss the tasks.

The Sincerity of Preaching to Strangers

Whenever you are in the presence of strangers, it is essential to recognize the power of hospitality. Whatever happened to genuine hospitality in the local congregation? You can often tell a lot about a church by how they treat their visitors. In today's culture, I've noticed that when a visitor tries to shake hands, people's eyes tend to wander elsewhere, looking at somebody else. We may do this because the heart performs out of habit rather than genuine warmth. Peter teaches us how to practice hospitality: "*Above all, keep loving one another earnestly, since love covers a multitude of sins. Show hospitality to one another without grumbling.*" (1 Pet 4:8–9). True hospitality in the church begins with legitimate leadership. It is impossible to lead with the heart of God unless you share the heart of God. If one does not have a vision for hospitality, they will never see the value or reality of being God's earthly agent. Hospitality must be in your heart before it can happen in your home. Everybody is not a disciple, but they can be. If I'm going to reach strangers, I must be open to other strangers.

If we don't make newcomers feel welcome, there's probably a nearby church with false doctrine that will make them feel comfortable and right at home. Would you return to a place where you did not feel welcome? The truth is, either we are connected or disconnected from the strangers in our pews. We are called to extend God's grace to others, just as He did for us when we were strangers. I have witnessed that some people are made to feel like strangers because we have unwittingly, or sometimes intentionally, labeled them as such. Don't kill the stranger; save the stranger and disciple them. In the end, there will be no excuses heard for your nonperformance to fulfill this vital aspect of ministry. Our response is a direct reflection of our faithfulness to God's call to love and hospitality.

Disciple-making Among Wolves

Disciple-making is a challenging and often tedious task. Matthew writes the words of Jesus,

> Behold, I am sending you out as sheep in the midst of wolves, so be wise as serpents and innocent as doves. Beware of men, for they will deliver you over to courts and flog you in their synagogues, and you will be dragged before governors and kings for my sake, to bear witness before them and the Gentiles (Matt 10:16–18).

The words are clear: Jesus is sending us into a world

filled with wolves eager to attack and destroy. Wolves are very dangerous creatures that can easily cause harm. Yet, Jesus also teaches us how to handle the wolves, not if, but when we encounter them. Preparation and wisdom are key to surviving and thriving in such environments. So, how did the church, which in Acts chapter 2 was a vibrant, growing community committed to, come to face such opposition today? One reason is a "Loss of Focus." Focus is the engine that drives everything. If you lose your spiritual focus, you'll lose your spiritual momentum.

Another reason for the decline in evangelistic efforts lies in our methodologies. Many churches prefer to be entertained rather than educated, often abandoning the mission of making disciples. A true disciple is someone who is growing spiritually, maturing in the Scriptures, and living as a student of Christ. A strong disciple is a prepared disciple. Preparation comes through:

- Never neglecting daily prayer,
- Never neglecting daily Bible reading, and
- Never letting a day go by without doing something for Jesus.

Despite opposition and persecution, we must continue to proclaim Christ. Your personal evangelistic efforts, your words, your life, and your love are vital in making disciples. In ministry, we must be ready to combat error at every opportunity. Paul writes to Timothy, *"You then, my child, be strengthened by the grace that is in Christ Jesus, and what you have heard from me in the presence of many witnesses entrust to faithful men, who will be able to teach others also"* (2 Tim 2:1–2). Don't let life's persecutions hinder your efforts to disciple others. A true disciple of Christ cares for the lost, seeks to right societal wrongs, worships God with his money and energy, and witnesses for Christ in every possible way. If we fail to commit to the mission and to the people of Christ, disciple-making will become unbalanced. Our world, community, and congregation would flourish much more if we devoted ourselves to helping others come to the knowledge and love of our Lord.

Chapter 3
Make the Bible Walk

THE BIBLE IS NOT a dead book, despite how some may portray it. The most effective way to capture and hold your audience's attention is to learn how to make the Bible come alive. Many years ago, when I attended International Bible College, now known as Heritage Christian University, the professors taught that every sermon we preach should be brought to life before our listeners. The cliché was to either put some fire in your sermon or put your sermon in the fire. In the book titled *The Art and Craft of Preaching*, Herbert Lockyer warns, "Preachers should avoid being sesquipedalian: someone who is long winded and overuses big words. Your audience may assume that you're smart, even if they don't really understand what you are saying" (1975, 48). As a minister of the gospel of Christ, your primary responsibility is to remind and warn others about what the Word says. You are like a carpenter, and God's Word is your set of tools. If a carpenter knows that his work will be inspected, he doesn't cut corners. Similarly, misusing or misapplying the Bible can lead to further ungodliness and confusion. If you're going to be effective in making the Bible walk, then you must be willing to dedicate serious study time. You cannot offer a remedy until you understand the cause. The power to breathe life into Scripture comes through diligent preparation and a sincere desire to see the Word become a living, breathing influence in your ministry and in the hearts of your listeners.

Preaching Is Giving the Bible a Voice

The pulpit is not a place for a preacher to argue his own selfish point or laypeople's terminology; I'm going to straighten them out. I've been to many congregations where the preacher spends more time arguing with one person from the pulpit. Those who come to service expect to hear a word from God, not to listen to ranting and raving about a situation that didn't go their way. A minister's first commitment is to God, and secondarily to His people. This world is full of people who are not committed to God. It's remarkable how we are committed to our jobs, sports, recreation, and other activities, but often neglect to make a strong commitment to grow and work for God.

The reason the church struggles to make a greater impact in our society is simple: many have made a decision about Christ but have not committed to Christ. When an airplane is on the runway, there comes a moment when the pilot will pull the lever for takeoff. Sadly, today, many churches contain members who have never truly launched because the preached sermon never comes alive to them. To be effective in any endeavor, commitment is essential. If God's Word is to reach a lost and dying world, then we as His disciples must make the Bible come alive at every opportunity we have.

Preaching for God Requires Commitment

As ministers of the gospel of Jesus Christ, we have been given a charge by God to teach and preach the Word. Paul instructs young Timothy to *"Preach the word; be ready in season and out of season; reprove, rebuke, and exhort, with complete patience and teaching"* (2 Tim 4:2). One major reason many believers and ministers struggle with commitment is laziness and the reluctance to study and fulfill the mission work that God has called them to do. I often remind my preaching colleagues that while many are lazy in serving God, what if God were lazy in blessing us with His daily grace? Preaching, serving, and living for Christ is a daily commitment. Whether we realize it or not, someone is listening to what we preach every day. People are paying attention to our media posts, what we say in stores, in community conversations, and beyond. We must prepare ourselves daily to point others to Jesus. The Great Commission is fundamentally about making a commitment. As Matthew writes, *"Go therefore and make disciples of all nations, baptizing them in the name of the Father and of the Son and of the Holy Spirit, teaching them to observe all that I have commanded you. And behold, I am with you always, to the end of the age"* (Matt 28:18–20). History reminds us: it doesn't take a large number of people to change the world —just a few committed individuals. There are two common reasons why many do not fully commit:

1. Fear of Responsibility: Your commitment defines your life.

- There are many dreamers in this world, but nothing happens until you wake up from your dream and start working.

- At some point, you must take responsibility for your own growth and development. Paul writes, *"Do your best to present yourself to God as one approved, a worker who has no need to be ashamed, rightly handling the word of truth"* (2 Tim 2:15).

2. Fear of Accountability: Some hide their talents and refuse to fully commit to what God has entrusted to them.

- A life of uncommitted devotion to God communicates that nothing truly godly matters to me.
- I've learned that long-term commitment pays off.
- Your entire life is the sum total of what you are committed to.

Winning others to Christ involves at least five tips for commitment and dedication:

1. True commitment is not a Sunday-only thing; It's a 24/7/365 type of commitment. John writes the words of Jesus, *"You did not choose me, but I chose you and appointed you that you should go and bear fruit and that your fruit should abide, so that whatever you ask the Father in my name, he may give it to you"* (John 15:16).
2. Be committed to talking about God to others.
3. Support your local church with love, prayers, attendance, and finances. Ministries do not develop by themselves; they require unwavering commitment.

4. Your level of commitment directly shapes your life. Tell me what you're committed to, and I will tell you where you're headed.
5. Always be prepared with the Word.

Spiritual Growth Assessment

As you reflect on your personal spiritual journey, ask yourself: where do you rank on the chart of spiritual growth? Just as a parent regularly checks on a child's development, we should assess our spiritual growth monthly and yearly. Paul writes in Colossians

> *And so, from the day we heard, we have not ceased to pray for you, asking that you may be filled with the knowledge of his will in all spiritual wisdom and understanding, so as to walk in a manner worthy of the Lord, fully pleasing to him: bearing fruit in every good work and increasing in the knowledge of God; being strengthened with all power, according to his glorious might, for all endurance and patience with joy; giving thanks to the Father, who has qualified you to share in the inheritance of the saints in light* (Col 1:9-12).

Our assessment of spiritual growth is influenced by both our feelings and our understanding of God's Word. Paul's prayer for the Colossians was for them to be filled with the knowledge of God's will. Our walk with God should be purposeful and deliberate, grounded in the continual strengthening that comes from Him. This strength in God will enable us to endure trials during turbulent times. It also prepares us to mentor others, just as God has mentored us. True spiritual growth is a lifelong journey of becoming more like Christ and deepening our understanding of His will.

Preaching Pushes Us to Get on the Ball

To be the best we can be for God, it requires gathering biblical information rooted in facts and preserving what we've read and studied. Effectiveness in any congregation depends on understanding the dos and don'ts of ministry. Herbert Lockyer also provides a helpful list of "The Preacher's Don'ts" in his book (1975, 114–118):

- Don't take sides —Never unless right and justified.
- Don't think that the church revolves around you as its owner.
- Don't think that because your plans and methods worked well in your last congregation will work in another.
- Don't be jealous of your predecessor or imagine that they accomplished nothing or knew nothing.
- Don't imagine that the new place is so very new. Folks are folks everywhere.
- Don't preach at people; always preach to them.
- Don't allow another preacher to abuse your people. Allow no one to destroy your good influence.
- Don't lose heart if results are scarce. Leave the outcome of your work with God.
- Don't have roast the preacher for dinner. If you cannot speak well of other preachers, say nothing at all.

- Don't forget that life and conduct count far more than your sermon.
- Don't forget that you are first a Christian, then a preacher.
- Don't forget to pray, love your Bible, and live near to your Master.
- Don't forget that at the judgment seat, your work will be tried by fire.

Many preachers are simply letting life pass them by. To live a productive life, whether in business, marriage, or ministry, requires us to get on the ball. Paul also writes in Colossians, "*Whatever you do, work heartily, as for the Lord and not for men, knowing that from the Lord you will receive the inheritance as your reward. You are serving the Lord Christ*" (Col 3:23-24).

Paul reminds us that we have a choice: either enjoy and labor effectively, or waste altogether. Success depends on how much effort *YOU* decide to put in. Your work ethic has the power to produce positive or negative results in your life. I remember during my school days, playing basketball, the coach's constant demand was: "Get On The Ball." If you didn't get on the ball when it was loose, it told him that you didn't want it badly enough, and he would pull you out of the game. To truly get on the ball as God's ministers, we must put our hearts into everything we do for Him. Every word spoken and every action taken should bring honor and glory to Christ. God requires your best, and it's time to match your practice with your potential.

Becoming a Good Steward in God's Production

Stewardship is about becoming a manager or someone

in authority under the owner. A good steward is willing to take control of their body and manage it responsibly. This is an area where many in the religious arena often neglect. It's difficult to serve God when your body is not functioning properly. Constant tiredness, sickness, fatigue, and mental health challenges can hinder your ability to be the best minister you can be. God expects us to take good care of our bodies. We must show our bodies love and not neglect them. Equally important is monitoring our spiritual abilities. If a spiritual person does not develop or cultivate their God-given gifts, those gifts become of little value.

A good steward also manages their possessions wisely. Making sound financial decisions with what God has entrusted to you can either help or hinder your ministry. Many preachers struggle financially because they fail to practice godly wisdom when it comes to managing money. Financial mismanagement can lead to bondage. It's easy to fall into terrible debt before you realize it. If you can't pay your bills, you may borrow more, sinking deeper into debt. It feels good to be free from the burden of debt, and God refers to those who fail to pay their debts as wicked. David writes in Psalms, "*The wicked borrows but does not pay back, but the righteous is generous and gives*" (Ps 37:21). If you want to experience the joy of being debt-free, be prepared to make sacrifices. Make a list of all your debts and prioritize paying off the smallest ones first. Apply any extra income toward debt repayment. Avoid unnecessary shopping, even if you receive a raise. Spend wisely, and do your best to avoid creating new debts. Learn to be content with what you have. God blesses us so that we can be a blessing to others.

Finally, be a good steward of your soul. It is important

to seek God and to save yourself. Your gift within the body of Christ is meant to edify, build up, and encourage others in doing the work of God. People don't plan to fail; they fail to plan. No one truly desires to fail in this life or the next, but neglecting stewardship can cost us dearly both personally and spiritually. Our families and our congregations suffer when we neglect our responsibilities because of a lack of accountability. If we allow God to lead us, we will achieve the results He desires. Stop hindering His work by continuing to do what we want instead of doing what He requires. An old proverb states, "*We are doomed to repeat the same lesson over and over until we get it right.*" How many people do we know who have repeated patterns in life? Gain wisdom and share it with others who cross your path.

Allowing God to Work in You

When you allow God to work on and in you, you are better off alone than to compromise with the devil. You don't have to make deals with the devil; by refusing to compromise, you can eliminate much stress and misery from your life. Paul writes, "*for it is God who works in you, both to will and to work for his good pleasure*" (Phil 2:13). Always be willing to grow. Never reach a point in life when you think you no longer need the truth. We have a free will choice to live however we want. God will not force anything on us. He is always working to bring about His good pleasure for the church. It is essential that we keep our zeal, our enthusiasm, by staying excited and committed to the work of God.

An object at rest tends to stay at rest, while an object in motion tends to stay in motion. Once you start moving in the direction of God, He will help you make any necessary adjustments along the way. We serve a God who has a plan for your increase and growth in life. But know this: every increase comes with challenges. Every door that God opens may not come easily. The bigger the door, the greater the challenge. The more God blesses you, the more enemies and problems you might face. You may not walk smoothly through every door, but be strong because your challenges might simply be signposts that you're on the right path.

My struggles remind me that God keeps me on His mind. Paul writes in Galatians, *"And let us not grow weary of doing good, for in due season we will reap, if we do not give up"* (Gal 6:9). Stop speaking defeat over your life. Monitor the words that come from your mouth and declare who you are in Christ.

- I am what the Bible says that I am.
- I am more than a conqueror (Rom 8:37).
- I am the head and not the tail (Deut 28:13).
- I can do what the Bible says I can do.
- I can do all things through Christ who gives me the strength (Phil 4:13).
- I have what the Bible says I have.

Furthermore, you have authority through Christ to trample on snakes and scorpions and to overcome all the power of the enemy; nothing shall harm you (Luke 10:19). Your relationship with God is your most important relationship you will ever have. When you get that relationship right, everything else will fall into place.

Chapter 4
Preaching that Meets the Needs of the People

THE CHURCH BENEFITS GREATLY from a preacher who knows how to effectively communicate. True impact occurs when a preacher has a clear vision in his conversation and his words are directed toward meeting the real needs of his audience. Just because a preacher is speaking from the pulpit doesn't mean that everyone is listening or truly understanding what's being said. As Christians, we communicate to the world in three primary ways: Through our

- Conduct,
- Conversation, and
- Culture.

How often do the saints of God keep the good news (*euangelion*) to themselves? Godly communication is vital for exchanging spiritual information, reducing strife and confusion, and fostering healthy relationships.

When something is particularly important, the devil often attempts to use misunderstanding to turn hearts away from God. To meet the needs of your listeners effectively, you must first understand who they are. Studying your audience is essential. Does your sermon address someone who has lost a loved one? Someone recently laid off from work? Someone going through a divorce? Someone struggling with wayward children? Or someone facing serious health challenges? Your message may not connect if it doesn't relate to where they are in their spiritual lives.

As James Daane notes in *Preaching with Confidence*, "When the pulpit is on the decline, the church is on the decline. When preaching is in crisis, the church is in crisis" (1980, 7). Meeting the needs of your listeners requires soaking in, meditating on, and immersing yourself in the Word of God. Walter S. Thomas once said in a sermon that "The power of narrative preaching lies in addressing the human situation." Preaching is both an art and a science; art in how we deliver our message, and it is the science in the content of what we communicate. When a preacher's goal is to truly meet the needs of his audience, his preaching will have a powerful impact, capable of turning the world upside down. Dr. Otis Moss once said in a sermon, "Look, listen, hear, and learn from all experiences of God's people." Connecting with members requires genuine engagement, listening to their stories, understanding their struggles, and learning how God is working in their lives.

Getting the Message from the Pulpit to the Pew

In my 30 years of preaching the gospel, I've had many people approach me on any given Sunday, saying, "I have a sermon on my heart that I would like to preach someday."

I usually observe the activity of these future ministers to see if they follow through, and many times, they leave the congregation a month later. What happened? I thought they had a message, a desire to share what God placed on their hearts. To effectively preach from the pulpit to the pew, God must call the messenger. The epidemic of ministers falling into disguise or failure is widespread. Therefore, one of the first questions any new preacher should ask himself is: Why preach?

Paul answers this question: *"For our appeal does not spring from error or impurity or any attempt to deceive, but just as we have been approved by God to be entrusted with the gospel, so we speak, not to please man, but to please God who tests our hearts"* (1 Thes 1:3–4). I often ask new preachers, How do you determine the central idea of your message? More often than not, they are unsure. The key to discovering the main idea of your message involves three steps:

1. Study the text thoroughly
2. Structure the text logically
3. Generate a clear subject or central theme.

The purpose of any sermon may be any of the following: it may be to inform, explain, persuade, encourage, inspire, entertain a particular subject, to correct, to call, to confront, to change, or to motivate toward a specific goal. Whatever the purpose, it must be rooted in a sincere calling from God, driven by a desire to serve His people, and aimed at producing spiritual growth and transformation.

Building Rapport with the Audience

Creating receptivity in your audience begins with forming genuine relationships. The success of reaching people hinges on having a clear vision of what can be accomplished through effective communication. Evangelism is about meeting the needs of individuals while communicating the gospel.

Dr. Alvin A. Low, in *Clearing the Fog*, outlines "The Twelve Commandments of Building Rapport" (2000, 72–73):

1. You shall respect your audience.
2. Whenever possible, you should meet with members of your audience before your talk.
3. You should start on time.
4. When possible, you should bestow small presents to your members.
5. You should maintain good eye contact with individuals, avoiding the temptation to scan your audience.
6. You should attempt to learn and use some of your members' own buzz words, acronyms, and jargon whenever possible, and of course, acknowledge your members by name.
7. You shall convey appreciation. Nothing connects two people better than a sincere compliment.
8. You should use breaks to continue nurturing rapport and socialize with your members.
9. You should seek feedback, especially on issues that affect your audience, such as room

temperature, volume level, and the speed of
your talk.

10. You should praise your members and make
    them heroes.

11. You should learn to be a good listener: give
    good eye contact, pause, listen to the entire
    statement, and never make a joke about your
    member's comment.

12. You should mirror your member's speaking
    patterns.

Building rapport is essential to creating a welcoming
and engaging environment. When people feel valued and
understood, they are more receptive to the message you
share.

Building Rapport Involves Removing the Barriers

What asked what makes his church more effective, a
thriving minister responded that he dedicates a significant
amount of time to removing internal, cultural, and
language barriers within his congregation. Paul illustrates
this principle *"To the weak I became weak, that I might win the
weak. I have become all things to all people, that by all means I
might save some"* (1 Cor 9:22). Elmer Towns, in *Winning the
Winnable*, emphasizes the importance of understanding
and adapting to the dialects of others: "To build rapport
with our congregation, we must be willing to learn another's person's dialect. There are diverse speaking groups in
America, and there is a barrier between both Christians
and the unsaved" (1989, 37–38). Christians desire for the
unsaved to bond with us right away. We want them to feel
they belong. But I've learned that if they don't feel like

they fit in, they will eventually drop out. Removing barriers, whether cultural or internal, creates a bridge for genuine relationships and effective ministry.

Be a Lively Preacher that Awakens the Spiritual Dead

Dead men do not wake the dead; consequently, our sermons should be lively and dynamic. If a man cannot be passionate about the Word of God, he has no business preaching. Every sermon should be preached as though it were our last. The preacher's primary task is to preach the Word. Paul writes to his young protégé Timothy

> I charge you in the presence of God and of Christ Jesus, who is to judge the living and the dead, and by his appearing and his kingdom: preach the word; be ready in season and out of season; reprove, rebuke, and exhort, with complete patience and teaching. For the time is coming when people will not endure sound teaching, but having itching ears they will accumulate for themselves teachers to suit their own passions and will turn away from listening to the truth and wander off into myths. As for you, always be sober-minded, endure suffering, do the work of an evangelist, fulfill your ministry (2 Tim 4:1–5).

Today, many pulpits have lost their passion for preaching. The secret to powerful preaching is knowing that God is at work within your life. The Bible is not dull, and your preaching should never be dull. Alex Montoya, in *Preaching with Passion*, reminds us: "If we are to lead souls to Heaven, then we must be those who descend from Heaven with God's Shekinah around us" (2007, 27).

Many preachers stumble in ministry because they don't

practice what they preach. If the sermon feeds your soul, it will feed others. A sermon is not merely an exercise in exegesis; it is a declaration of a truth meant to inspire moral action. To preach with passion, one must preach with power, energy, and drive. Without passion, a sermon becomes nothing more than a lecture.

The Power of Unity

Many Christians prefer to live their lives in a very private way; they don't want anyone meddling in their personal affairs. However, to help others overcome their adversarial moments, we need strong fellowship and unity with one another. The more fellowship we share, the more we are perfected in Jesus. A box of crayons can teach us a great deal about Christian unity and fellowship. Some crayons are sharp, some are pretty, and some are dull. Some crayons have unusual names, and others are used to their fullest potential. Yet, all of them must learn to live in the same box (the church). If crayons can get along, then surely Christians can too.

There is a significant difference between being united with one another and being untied. This distinction lies in the reversal of just two letters: unity versus untied. Unity is for our personal benefit; it nurtures, flavors, and benefits the church. You can choose to be a part of the problem or part of the solution. Unity also makes us much more effective as Christians. We are stronger and more impactful when we work together. Two can accomplish more, and three can accomplish even faster. Imagine what our community and the world would look like if everyone worked together in unity. God values unity above all. A team of horses moving in the same direction can achieve far more than one pulling in opposite directions. God's work is best done through teamwork. After all, there is no "I" in team. Unity is the tool that reflects Christ's love and extends it into the world.

If we ever needed unity in the church, it's right now. Every man and woman should examine their life concerning unity in the body of Christ, because it's God's desire that we live in harmony. It's strange that the world can often get along better than we do in the church. They invite us to their party and functions, yet it's exceedingly rare that we invite them to our church events. The reason we may hesitate to invite others could be due to a lack of unity among believers. David writes, *"Behold, how good and pleasant it is when brothers dwell in unity"* (Ps 133:1). Let's take a look at the positive effects that come from unity:

- Unity keeps us focused on a common goal.
- Unity is not about fighting; it's about delighting in each other.
- Unity fosters a joyful spirit in our relationships.
- Unity is greater than any preacher's preaching.
- Unity surpasses the importance of singing, vision, ministry, or even church buildings.
- Unity exceeds the influence of any church staff, deacons, trustees, members, or ushers.

Keynotes

- If we do not work together, nothing of lasting significance will be accomplished.
- The test of unity is not whether you can agree with somebody.

- The test of unity is not whether you can find someone to do what you want.
- The true test of unity is how well you stick with those whom God has called you to serve and be part of.

Work for God and He Will Promote You

Everyone desires promotion in life, whether in career, relationships, or spiritual growth. There are two kinds of promotion: natural and supernatural. Natural promotion comes from human effort and acknowledgment, while supernatural promotion comes from God Himself. Man can promote you one day and demote you the next. The word *promote* means to lift, elevate, or upgrade. When you trust in God, He can promote you in every area, financially, spiritually, physically, and emotionally.

Many people allow financial struggles to hold them back from experiencing the greater blessings God has in store. For the Christian, maintaining the right attitude towards money is crucial. An improper attitude can cause us to lose our family, health, friendship, and even our relationship with God. Just one wrong step, headed in the wrong direction, can disrupt us mentally, physically, and spiritually, affecting us not only for this life but for eternity. Many Christians have lost their smile, joy, sanity, and peace because they ignored God's guidance and connected with the wrong people. If you work faithfully for God, trusting Him and following His leadership, He will elevate you at the right time. Remember, your promotion is ultimately in His hands. Stay committed, stay humble, and keep your right attitude, because God's desire is to lift you in His perfect timing.

Stay with God and Keep the Right Attitude

You have heard the saying before: Your attitude determines your altitude, which ultimately affects your blessings. Many ministers desire the blessings that come from God but are unwilling to make the necessary adjustments. If change were easy, everyone would be doing it. James MacDonald, in *Lord, Change My Attitude*, declares, "Gratitude is the attitude that sets the attitude for my living" (2001, 73).

Spiritual balance needs to be restored in every Christian's life. Craig Groeschel, in *#Struggles*, emphasizes, "Your identity comes from who you are following. Are you following Jesus as we live in a selfie-centered world?" (2015, 91) Below are some key perspectives from both authors about attitudes:

- A complaining attitude is an unchecked attitude. A constant complainer will reap the consequences of his complaints.
- A thankful attitude is the pathway to a man's wholeness.
- A covetous attitude is one who is infected with materialism. Enough is never enough.
- A contentment attitude is simply being satisfied with God's sufficient provision.
- A critical attitude destroys our relationship with others and ruins our fellowship with God. People will criticize everything about you due to their critical attitude.
- A loving attitude will cover a multitude of sins. When Christ is all you have, you will finally realize that Christ is all you need.

- A doubting attitude is when there is an absence of faith. Your circumstances in life will either shrink or stretch your faith.
- A faith attitude is an attitude that is rooted in a God who is real.

Maintaining the right attitude keeps you aligned with God's purpose and positions for blessings and spiritual growth.

Principles for Answering the Call

Answering the call of God is not always what you initially envisioned. Your life is a series of choices, not mere chances. Every decision to go in a specific direction can influence your life for the next twenty years or more. Because of this, preparation is absolutely essential for a successful ministry. That preparation must include both experience and education, as God needs to shape you into what He desires. In ministry, you must learn how to shift from living an emotional life to living a God-centered life. How can one accomplish this great transition? Consider these principles.

- You must continually strive to become like Jesus, who is your greatest example of an excellent minister.
- You must obey the same principles that are set forth in God's Word that you expect everyone else to obey, even when your mind does not understand.
- You must continue to hold on to those embedded principles that you once learned,

knowing they are the very underpinnings of the durable foundation upon which you have built your life and ministry.

- Do all you can within your power to make the gospel relevant and to love the lost.
- The ministry has no place for a vulnerable ego. A wise man once said: Good understanding in the front makes no misunderstanding in the rear.
- Always understand that you are on a God assignment, and He will always provide.

Walking in obedience to these principles will help you answer God's call with integrity and purpose, positioning you for His divine best.

Chapter 5
The Call to Preach Is also the Call to Prepare

IF YOU DO NOT PREPARE your sermon thoroughly, people will not take your words or message seriously. If your character is flawed, then your message will be flawed as well. As a minister of the gospel of Christ, you must live an exemplary life. The words of the preacher, both in the pulpit and outside of it, are critically important. Thorough research will help make your sermon powerful and effective. Thomas Holland, in *Steps Into the Pulpit*, writes:

> The lawyer has a method in getting ready for a case. The medical doctor has a method for the diagnosis of illness. The scientist has a method for verifying or rejecting hypothesis. The preacher should have a method for gathering information for a sermon (1988, 85).

I remember when I first entered the ministry, asking a seasoned preacher for tips on how to craft a lesson. After listening to his sermon, I quickly realized that his message was rooted in distorted theology. Paul teaches about a distorted theology in the book of Galatians,

I am astonished that you are so quickly deserting him who called you in the grace of Christ and are turning to a different gospel—not that there is another one, but there are some who trouble you and want to distort the gospel of Christ. But even if we or an angel from heaven should preach to you a gospel contrary to the one we preached to you, let him be accursed. As we have said before, so now I say again: If anyone is preaching to you a gospel contrary to the one you received, let him be accursed (Gal 1:6–9).

Teams in sports understand the true meaning of practice. Likewise, the man of God must grasp the true meaning of being prepared. Proper sermon rehearsal includes expository content, evangelistic purpose, enthusiastic presentation, and consistent life exemplification. One must earn the right to stand in the pulpit. If the preacher is not prepared, the older generation used to have a saying: "It'll all come out in the wash."

Robb Thompson, in *Excellence in Ministry*, provides us with a list of principles essential for preparing for God's calling (2002, 49–50):

- An excellent minister understands that God has already scheduled his moment for separation unto the call, but must ready himself for that moment.
- An excellent minister pursues the change that will prepare him for the future.
- An excellent minister chooses to dismantle his life in times when he can withstand the pain of change.
- An excellent minister embraces short-term denial in order to create long-term benefits.

- An excellent minister understands that lasting change requires rooting out yesterday's pain in order to experience relief from yesterday's memories.
- An excellent minister always builds his life on a firm foundation.
- An excellent minister lives life by his principles, not by his emotions.
- An excellent minister knows that testing is required for promotion.
- An excellent minister knows that today's excellence is tomorrow's mediocrity.
- An excellent minister is convinced that every step away from temptation is one step closer to God's dream within him.
- An excellent minister knows that obedience to the known will of God is the key to unlocking His unknown will.
- An excellent minister establishes God's principles in his life one step at a time.
- An excellent minister uses focus to deliver him to his God-given destination.
- An excellent minister cannot determine the time of his promotion, but he can prepare for his reception of it.
- An excellent minister understands that promotion comes from God, but its timing is in the hands of men.

Preach God's Word and Not Your Opinion

A good preacher knows exactly what his congregation needs because he is in tune with the members and leaders of the church. Derek Morris, in *Powerful Biblical Preaching*, emphasizes, "If you are a visiting preacher for a congregation, one needs to go online and view their services so he can get a good feel of the congregation" (2005, 35). The most dangerous mistake a minister can make is to preach his opinion rather than faithfully deliver the Word of God. Growing spiritually involves faithfully attending as many positive spiritual functions as possible. This keeps your mind focused and your soul nourished.

If your car started only one out of three times, would you call that faithful? If you didn't show up to work three times a week, would your boss consider you reliable? Paul provides us with a solution to nourish our souls, "*So faith comes from hearing, and hearing through the word of Christ*" (Rom 10:17). I am reminded of a preacher who stayed in the home of an elder who didn't open his Bible all week. The preacher asked how he could lead the flock of God without hearing from Him. It made me wonder how can any preacher desire to lead, counsel, and teach others when they haven't prepared themselves to hear from God? In preparing to preach, develop an intentional attitude towards the text. Allow it to shape your heart and mind before you deliver it to others.

Wrestling with the Text

God's Word is meant to be spoken and heard. Spoken words carry power. Every minister studies and prepares differently, depending on their habits. While many preachers learn to preach through preaching manuals, others learn to preach by observation and participation. Cleophus Larue, in *More Power in the Pulpit*, notes, "In the Black Church, one does not learn how to become a Black preacher; one learns how to become a preacher in the Black religious experience" (1989, 33).

Preaching is incredibly potent in our congregations today. You can control the message and the words that are spoken. But you cannot control the meaning that develops in the minds of your listeners. Wrestling with the text allows one to really listen for God and to rightly divide the Word of God. Pattern theology involves examining the sacred text to identify established patterns throughout scripture. When wrestling with the text, pay attention to what was done, how often it was done, and in what manner. God is a God of pattern. Scripture informs and shapes our theological convictions. Henry Mitchell reminds us: "Folks will do what they celebrate" (1989, 64). If you don't celebrate fully while wrestling with the text, your congregation won't either. It's imperative that the man of God master the scripture. The text is often the most powerful part of your sermon. The congregation will forgive a preacher for not speaking correct English, grammar mistakes, or improper use of pronouns. Attire may also be forgiven. But what cannot be forgiven is the preacher's lack of knowledge of the scriptures.

It's not the quantity of reading that matters most, but the quality. Dr. Frank E. Ray advises: "The preacher ought to have a gallery and a garden. You ought to have a gallery (a library) where you commune with the wisdom of the ages. You ought to have a garden where you can pull up plants from your own experience." Paul emphasizes the importance of this, *"For if I preach the gospel, that gives me no ground for boasting. For necessity is laid upon me. Woe to me if I do not preach the gospel!"* (1 Cor 9:16) To wrestle effectively with the text, the preacher must identify the main parts of the text, the tension that exists in the text, and how it influences the characters' thoughts and actions. When this is done well, your sermon should come alive through connection and celebration.

Defining Your Gift

God has placed a unique gift or talent within every person, and the world will make room for it. Your talent is the spiritual gift that will enable you to fulfill your vision. A preacher will find true fulfillment, purpose, and contentment in his work when he utilizes what God has given him. If you are intelligent but are not exercising your gift, you're probably going to be poor in spirit and life. If you're educated but haven't developed your talent, you may find yourself depressed, frustrated, and exhausted. The world won't move over for you just because you're smart. Your God-given spiritual gift is the key to your success in life and in ministry.

Anyone who discovers his or her gift, develops it, and makes it will become a valuable asset. Do what you were born to do, because that is where you will find your true livelihood. No matter how big the world is, there is a place for you. There is a place for you when you discover and manifest your gift. Often, we worry about the rights and wrongs of other people more than we do our own sins and shortcomings. The most destructive sin in your life right now is likely the one you're most defensive about. God created you for the purpose of His Kingdom going forward. He has equipped you to reach people that no one else can.

Godly men do not need labels to validate that they are workers for God. Being a minister is much more than a title; it describes one's work as God has given him a unique gift. A gift is something that someone gave you that you didn't have to pay for. The first step towards opening doors for your gift is to ensure that it belongs to you. You cannot grow a gift that isn't truly yours. Discover your gift, acknowledge it, embrace it, and own it.

Standing in the Gap for God

Today's culture calls for more men of God who are willing to stand in the gap for the nation, the community, and the church. Ezekiel emphasizes the importance of this role.

> *The people of the land have practiced extortion and committed robbery. They have oppressed the poor and needy, and have extorted from the sojourner without justice. And I sought for a man among them who should build up the wall and stand in the breach before me for the land, that I should not destroy it, but I found none. Therefore, I have poured out my indignation upon them. I have consumed them with the fire of my wrath. I have returned their way upon their heads, declares the Lord God* (Ezek 22:29–31).

We are the sum total of what others invest in us and what we choose to incorporate in our lives. Therefore, we should make up our minds to be the best Christians we can be; equipped with God's Word, vigilant over our mouths, committed to prayer and meditation, and guided by wise and godly mentors. You will never be an effective mentor to others until you're willing to receive honest, straight talk from your own mentors. You learn from others who are successful at what they do. Keep in mind that as you're looking up to someone for advice and encouragement, there is someone else who will be looking up to you.

What we do today as preachers will shape leaders of tomorrow. I've heard that Uncle Sam is looking for a few good men in the military. Will you be willing today to be that "spiritually good man" that God can count on? As the old proverb goes, "Give a man a fish and you feed him for a day; teach a man to fish and you feed him for a lifetime." Paul reminds us, *"For we are his workmanship, created in Christ Jesus for good works, which God prepared beforehand, that we should walk in them"* (Eph 2:10). God has deposited something in you that the world desperately needs.

The assignment of a preacher is considered to be threefold: to do, to teach, and to serve. You do the Word; you teach others to do it; and you serve. Constant prayer is vital as you stand in the gap for God. Prayer is not a waste of time; rather, it's an investment in your future. Prayer is also how we secure spiritual growth. The enemy attacks daily, trying to remind you of past mistakes that make you feel unworthy to serve or preach for God. But if you trust God, He will help you to recover from every error in your life. If you can't manage your mistakes, you will never reach where God is trying to take you. You will make mistakes, everyone does, but don't let a mistake turn you into a mistake. The game isn't over just because your shot was blocked. When you are wrong, own it. Admit it, learn from it, and move forward. The best of us mess up; the key is to stand daily in the gap for God.

To stand in the gap for God, you must be willing to stir up the inner strength of your mind and put on the whole armor of God in order to stand against various troubles, trials, and tribulations. We all face problems in life. You are either facing a problem, in the midst of a problem, or coming out of a problem. Throughout the Bible, we see that everyone faced struggles. Problems are inevitable, whether you're saved or not. Your problems will either allow you to release "fear" or "faith" in your life. Your words have power. You can rebuild your house, your ministry, your marriage, and your money based on the words that come from your mouth. Jesus confirms, "*I have said these things to you, that in me you may have peace. In the world you will have tribulation. But take heart; I have overcome the world*" (John 16:33).

Do not let the devil do all the talking in your life. When he speaks, speak back with God's Word. Controlling the words that come from your mouth is a matter of choice. Sadly, the enemy has conditioned many saints to talk negatively, and often, people will agree with you just to hush you up. But there must come a time when we learn from our struggles and mistakes. Struggles can be beneficial if we learn lessons that draw us closer to God. Sometimes, we find ourselves in struggles because of the choices we make. Our action often leads to pain, sorrow, humiliation, regret, shame, and guilt. Trust in God, stand in the gap for Him, and He will exalt you in due time.

Preparing to Make Disciples

Discipleship of Christ is the process of shaping someone to become like Christ, resulting in that person becoming a follower or student of Him. Discipleship of the devil is the process of turning someone into a devil worshipper. Demons are constantly active, and many people are influenced by them daily. You can often tell those who are of the devil by their walk, talk, and actions. If a person is not taught how to take control of the demon, the demon will quickly take control of that individual. The devil's primary goal is to dominate your life. God, on the other hand, desires us to be free and to teach others how to break free from the schemes of the enemy.

Jesus declares,

> *And Jesus came and said to them, "All authority in heaven and on earth has been given to me. Go therefore and make disciples of all nations, baptizing them in the name of the Father and of the Son and of the Holy Spirit, teaching them to observe all that I have commanded you. And behold, I am with you always, to the end of the age"* (Matt 28:18–20).

Christians must be equipped to fight the flesh, live by the Spirit, and develop leaders who will carry the message forward. Do not allow the devil to leave a destructive legacy in your family or community. Godly discipleship is vital because it brings true freedom into a person's life. God calls us to tell His story. If we fail to do so, the devil will fill the void and tell the story from his perspective.

Chapter 6
Pulpit Etiquette

A THOROUGH STUDY before preaching a lesson is essential because it benefits you in the present and contributes to your growth throughout life. It's not about how much we study; it's about how well we study that truly matters. If you want to study less, you must learn to study effectively. Your study environment plays a crucial role in how well you absorb information. The key to effective studying is taking good notes. The more you learn, the longer that knowledge stays with you. There are effective ways and poor ways to study. Learning can be enjoyable because God has given us a desire to gain knowledge and understanding. The act of learning stimulates the mind and keeps us growing intellectually. When we know how to study properly, it enhances our joy and elevates our pulpit etiquette to its highest level.

A good teaching method with select the text before stating a proposition, then extrapolating the sermon from that chosen text. The experience in the "Black Church" comes when the people from the pews encourage the man of God by saying, "make it plain, preacher," "you're preaching up there," or "stay right there, preacher." These are signals of a friendly, engaging conversation between the preacher and the hearers. What the listeners are expressing is their confidence that the man of God is preaching the unadulterated Word of God and encouraging him to keep going. To cultivate proper pulpit etiquette, the preacher must first be an authentic preacher or one who genuinely lives the message. James Harris, in *The Word Made Plain*, notes: "In many churches, there are hearers who wait until a certain transition in the sermon before they get involved. It is known as style switching due to a transition in tone and cadence" (2004, 94). Harris also emphasizes that: "The biblical text and the African American experience are the Black preacher's main tools for expounding on the Word of God. The context and the experience of the preacher play a role in understanding and interpretation of the text" (2004, 131).

Pulpit etiquette is particularly strong in the Black church, where culture influences interpretation and hermeneutics. Black homiletic preaching focuses on the power and effectiveness of communication. Henry Mitchell, in *Black Preaching*, expresses: "Perhaps the greatest evidence of the power of black preaching is that the black belief system of folk Christianity has kept its believers alive and coping, even when in an oppressed condition that would have crushed many believers" (1990, 34). A vital aspect of this powerful art includes storytelling. Every culture loves a relevant and engaging story. To tell a compelling story during a sermon, the preacher must embody all the roles involved and make the story come alive. When done skillfully, members of the audience feel as if they have seen the action firsthand and even participated in it. Mannerisms such as gestures, tone, variance, and rhythm are tools the preacher uses in order to add interest in the storytelling.

The highest honor on earth is the calling to preach the message of God. Don Dewelt, in *If You Want to Preach*, offers six fundamental principles for developing pulpit etiquette, which serve as helpful guides for weekly preparation (1957, 70–71). These principles are based on the six fundamental questions: what, who, why, when, where, and how.

1. **What**: Focuses on the characteristics or attributes of the subject.
2. **Who**: Identifies the person or people involved in the subject.
3. **Why**: Explores the reasons behind the subject.
4. **When**: Considers the timing or moment related to the subject.
5. **Where**: Looks at the location of the subject.
6. **How**: Examines the method or process of the subject.

Pulpit Etiquette Means Knowing Your God-Given Assignment

God requires services from the heart. You can attend church and preach weekly, but if your heart is not in it, your service is meaningless. A soldier's heart must be right, and preparation must be made before being sent out onto the battlefield for Uncle Sam. Likewise, in spiritual warfare, a believer must prove their faithfulness in the small tests before being entrusted with greater responsibilities. True service is an internal matter, not merely an external formality. Just as a military soldier needs basic training, God's soldiers also need foundational training. As a soldier for God, the world looks to the church and to those who are connected with God. If God is not moving in a people, they are not truly His church. The apostle Paul, in the book of Acts, depended on God to work powerfully through him as he sought others to teach him a clearer understanding of Jesus. In Paul states, "*I am a Jew, born in Tarsus in Cilicia, but brought up in this city, educated at the feet of Gamaliel according to the strict manner of the law of our fathers, being zealous for God as all of you are this day*" (Acts 22:3). Each of us has a life to live, a work to do, and opposition to face. Paul also teaches young Timothy that a good soldier must endure hardship. He says, "*Share in suffering as a good soldier of Christ Jesus. No soldier gets entangled in civilian pursuits, since his aim is to please the one who enlisted him*" (2 Tim 2:3–4). You can't enter a spiritual battle with a carnal mind.

You cannot stay focused on your divine assignment if you don't clearly understand what it is. Even if your assignment is challenging, God has equipped you spiritually to preserve you at all costs. You were created with a specific purpose: to fulfill a divine assignment and influence the world around you. What matters is not the duration of your life, but the donation of your life. Are you donating your time, efforts, and energy to the cause of Christ? Your purpose in life is to become what God has designed you to be. As Jesus said, "*I glorified you on earth, having accomplished the work that you gave me to do*." (John 17:4).

If You Roll with God, He Has the Last Words

While focusing on your pulpit etiquette, it's important to remind your audience that God has the final say. No man: your boss, your spouse, or the judge, will have the last word as long as God is seated on the throne. There will always be people willing to support you, so stop making excuses for why you're not fully committed to working for God.

I've heard people say, "You are what you eat," but that's not entirely accurate. The truth is, "You are what you digest." Many Christians have ingested the wrong things that are not aligned with God's Word. That's why it's crucial never to abandon your dreams, visions, or hope. God will always send someone to help support you on your journey.

Each of us should seek to find our purpose, follow it wholeheartedly, and finish it before leaving this world. Purpose is not merely about attending church and taking notes. I've known people who have taken notes religiously for years and still don't know their Bible. If God gave them an open-book test, they would likely fail. Whatever you were born to do, do it with all your might. You will eventually come to realize that you cannot outdo God, and you will always find grace for your race. Every preacher should learn how to maximize his purpose and potential while living in the land of the living.

Be Mindful of the Offended Christians in the Church

Non-spiritual Christians are often those who walk around feeling offended most of the time. These are the problematic ones who tend to destroy friendships and relationships. When a Christian becomes offended, it introduces division and toxicity into the church body. Paul warns in 2 Corinthians about how the devil works tirelessly: *"so that we would not be outwitted by Satan; for we are not ignorant of his designs."* (2 Cor 2:11). Offense is typically defined as a perceived violation or attack; an act or word that causes hurt, anger, bitterness, and resentment. When someone is offended, it can be exceedingly difficult for them to resolve the issue. The preacher's role is to teach the importance of reconciliation, how to work through these issues, and restore the relationship. Instead of healing and unity, many relationships become strained, and people often fake their emotions or avoid each other altogether.

Strife and offense should never compromise the quality of our relationship with fellow Christians. When someone is offended in the assembly, it often blocks their ability to interpret and receive God's word. Life can become frustrating if we take offense at every negative word or remark we hear. There will be times in your ministry when you must access the source of gossip or criticism. I have learned that when God's Word is hindered, it's often because members are so upset with one another that they leave the church altogether, and Satan is happy. Such actions blind members spiritually, causing them to make rash and unwise decisions. For example, a wife once became offended with her husband and, in her emotional turmoil, cut the tires from the family car. That rash act left no way for the family to go anywhere or even get to work. Similarly, a husband, offended by his wife, went on a drunken binge. Because of his actions, they could not pay their bills, which were already overdue. This was a costly mistake that worsened their situation. It's time for us to remember who we are in Christ and to our rightful place in the ministry for God's glory. We must guard our hearts, promote reconciliation, and refuse to let offense hinder the work of the Lord.

Pulpit Etiquette is Bringing All Men to the Knowledge of Truth

Benjamin Franklin once said, "An investment in knowledge pays the best interest." Knowledge is the foundation for growth and development. Without proper knowledge, success becomes stagnant. Hosea writes, *"My people are destroyed for lack of knowledge"* (Hos 4:6). Knowledge refers to the facts or practical understanding of a subject. When we understand the facts of life, we tend to do better. A person can only pursue what he knows. If someone does not know about God, how can they pursue Him? As preachers of the gospel, the more we dedicate ourselves to understanding God's Word, the more effectively we can communicate it to our listeners. Without proper knowledge, you will always live beneath your privilege.

Every person needs the gospel truth. Paul writes

> *Therefore, having this ministry by the mercy of God, we do not lose heart. But we have renounced disgraceful, underhanded ways. We refuse to practice cunning or to tamper with God's word, but by the open statement of the truth we would commend ourselves to everyone's conscience in the sight of God. And even if our gospel is veiled, it is veiled to those who are perishing. In their case the god of this world has blinded the minds of the unbelievers, to keep them from seeing the light of the gospel of the glory of Christ, who is the image of God* (2 Cor 4:1–4).

What good is a hidden gospel? It serves no purpose if kept concealed or no use to those who remain in darkness.

- Satan delights in blinding the minds of both God's children and the lost. Those who hear the gospel but refuse to allow it to penetrate their hearts remain in spiritual blindness.
- Satan prefers it when believers operate in unbelief. Many find it pleasing to rebel against God and His Word.
- Satan strives to keep as many possible uninterested in the gospel. An uninterested person is a spiritually perishing person. Humanity is perishing without Christ, while the gospel remains veiled to the lost.
- The gospel is hidden from individuals because of their own choices.

It is our responsibility to preach the gospel faithfully and continually strive to be the salt of the earth and the light of the world. We must make every effort to unveil the truth and lead others into the saving knowledge of Jesus Christ.

Pulpit Etiquette Means No Turning Back

As preachers, we currently see countless people turning away from God and His church. Many people have stopped reading the Bible, which once served as their primary source of encouragement. Many have ceased studying the Bible, which once developed their character. Others have stopped coming to church, not only to edify others but also to be edified themselves. Instead of turning to the Lord, they are now turning away from Him. You will often hear excuses about why people are no longer committed as they once were. The root of their turning back is often rooted in fostering a digital relationship instead of a genuine spiritual relationship with God. Google Church is on the rise. It offers a convenient way for those who lack time or opportunity to gain spiritual insight.

Many young non-Christians are turning away from traditional Christianity because they belong to the Google Church. Increasingly, young Christians abandon the true church and transfer their membership to online platforms. The church of Google can be dangerous because Dr. Google is not a theologian. Google expresses the opinions of believers, non-believers, those in and out of fellowship, false teachers, Buddhists, Muslims, Atheists, and many others. Google Church has become popular among those who do not want to take the time to rightly divide the Word of Truth. Authors David Kinnaman and Mark Matlock, in *Faith for Exiles*, describe "four kinds of people in the digital era of discipleship" (2019, 41–46).

1. *Prodigals*: These are the ex-Christians—22%. These are individuals who do not currently identify themselves as Christians. They are living a life similar to the prodigal son.
2. *Nomads*: These are the unchurched—30%. These are individuals who identify themselves as Christians but have not attended church in the past month and have not been actively involved in the past year.
3. *Habitual churchgoer*: They represent a 38% population. They attend church monthly but have no active engagement. They are generally the last ones in and the first ones out.

4. *Resilient disciples*: These are Christ followers who make up the 10% who faithfully attend worship, believe in the Bible, and do the work that God has called them to do.

The question is often asked of Christians: Are you a Fan or Follower? Today's culture has a different terminology that says I'm not committed to either. Followship is a different lingo in our day and time. People can follow you on Facebook, Twitter, Instagram, Snapchat, TikTok, and still not be true followers of Christ. Author Kyle Idleman, in *Not a Fan*, writes, "People never define their relationship with Jesus, which is known as the D.T.R. effect" (2011, 30-31). Defining the relationship determines your level of commitment. Commitment is when you want to see where things stand and whether what you have is real.

Jesus is seeking our decision and commitment today. John writes about Nicodemus,

> *Now there was a man of the Pharisees named Nicodemus, a ruler of the Jews. This man came to Jesus by night and said to him, "Rabbi, we know that you are a teacher come from God, for no one can do these signs that you do unless God is with him." Jesus answered him, "Truly, truly, I say to you, unless one is born again he cannot see the kingdom of God." Nicodemus said to him, "How can a man be born when he is old? Can he enter a second time into his mother's womb and be born?" Jesus answered, "Truly, truly, I say to you, unless one is born of water and the Spirit, he cannot enter the kingdom of God"* (John 3:1-5).

Nicodemus was willing to take his relationship to the next level. Being an admirer of Jesus costs nothing, but becoming a true follower comes with a price tag.

Nicodemus came to Jesus at night, avoiding the questions of the religious leaders and risking his reputation. If he had followed Jesus during the daytime, it could have cost him his influential position, respect from his co-workers, income, friendships, and family relationships. Has following Jesus cost you anything? Jesus didn't want Nicodemus only at night; He wanted him during the day as well. Luke writes the words of Jesus, "*If anyone would come after me, let him deny himself and take up his cross daily and follow me*" (Luke 9:23). The phrase "come after" is a term used of a romantic relationship or enthusiastically in pursuit of someone you love. Jesus is looking for three types of people, as Luke writes,

> "*As they were going along the road, someone said to him, "I will follow you wherever you go." And Jesus said to him, "Foxes have holes, and birds of the air have nests, but the Son of Man has nowhere to lay his head." To another he said, "Follow me." But he said, "Lord, let me first go and bury my father." And Jesus said to him, "Leave the dead to bury their own dead. But as for you, go and proclaim the kingdom of God." Yet another said, "I will follow you, Lord, but let me first say farewell to those at my home." Jesus said to him, "No one who puts his hand to the plow and looks back is fit for the kingdom of God"* (Luke 9:57–62).

- We should go with Jesus in the "wherever" moment (v 57–58). Wherever means no restrictions, no boundaries, and no borders. It is a journey of risks and uncertainty.
- We should go with Jesus in the "whenever" moment (v 59–60). You would think Jesus would understand this man's dilemma, but He accepts no excuses. The most dangerous part of

following Jesus, tomorrow is not what you will lose between now and then. The longer you put Him off, the more likely it is that following Him will never happen.

- We should go with Jesus in the "whatever" moment (v 61–62). Jesus breaks down the plowman's ship, expressing the need to give full attention to one's works. It's not that following Jesus wasn't important to this man, but following Jesus wasn't his top priority.

Are you willing to teach others to surrender to Jesus as you have?

Surrendering to Jesus requires no reserves, no retreats, and no regrets.

Chapter 7
Preaching with Conviction

As gospel preachers, we must understand that God's work is serious business. Unfortunately, society has reached a point where many no longer take God's Word seriously. We live in a culture filled with people who dwell in yesterday, having no clear plan for how to handle today. There is a distinct difference between the people of yesterday and the people of today. Those of yesterday often remember what you did, what you accomplished or failed at, and may try to pull you back to their version of the past. Conversely, the people of today are like scaffolds; they are there for you to build on. They push us forward and challenge us to grow.

To preach with conviction, one must recognize that God is in the process of reprogramming us for success as ministers. Joshua writes

Only be strong and very courageous, being careful to do according to all the law that Moses my servant commanded you. Do not turn from it to the right hand or to the left, that you may have good success wherever you go. This Book of the Law shall not

depart from your mouth, but you shall meditate on it day and night, so that you may be careful to do according to all that is written in it. For then you will make your way prosperous, and then you will have good success. Have I not commanded you? Be strong and courageous. Do not be frightened, and do not be dismayed, for the Lord your God is with you wherever you go (Josh 1:7–9).

One of the challenges in ministry is that we sometimes listen too much to the wrong voices. When we listen long enough to those who are not aligned with God's purpose, it will sap us of our energy and steal our joy. Every preacher, Christian, brother, sister, and member of every church everywhere needs to be reprogrammed by God. Preaching with conviction acts as a catalyst in this reprogramming process. When God reprograms your faith, you can then reprogram your family. When your family is reprogrammed, your finances will follow suit. We should teach others to allow God to reprogram them to learn how to be kind, loving, and faithful Christians. Conviction in preaching helps facilitate this divine reprogramming, empowering everyone to live according to God's purpose.

Benefits of a Programmed Life

The benefits of living a reprogrammed life by God far outweigh those living without Godly alignment. A reprogrammed life leads to a reprogrammed attitude. This is when one's attitude has become stronger than usual due to spending time with the Lord. When you know who God is and teach the realness of God, you get a "nevertheless" spirit. When God is for you, you don't worry about those who oppose you. The doctors may tell you that you have cancer in your body (nevertheless); your spouse may tell you that you can't live without them (a nevertheless moment); your employer may give you a pink slip on your job (nevertheless); You might have believed you couldn't feed or clothe your family, graduate high school, get that job, or live the life you're living now; nevertheless, God has reprogrammed your attitude for success.

Once God reprograms your attitude, He then begins to reprogram your actions. Your attitude can change, but if your actions remain the same, problems will persist. Surprisingly, many Christians know how to shout on Sunday but have no idea how to live after the benediction prayer is over. When we allow God to reprogram both our attitude and our actions, He begins to shift our agenda. He refocuses your vision and grants you the victory. Remarkable things happen when you allow God to be in charge. When He is leading, He fights your battles and makes your enemies your footstool. Victory in every area of your life belongs to you because He's in charge.

God Recruits from the Pit and Not the Pedestal

Where the world sees failure, God sees success. He found Gideon in a hole, Joseph in prison, and Daniel in the lion's den. Despite our mess, we are still qualified to be the salt and light of the world. Many churches today are not growing because they are considered spiritually unhealthy. Carey Nieuwhof, in *Lasting Impact*, explains, "The reason many preachers are not making an impact is due to many of us are focused on our wants, preferences, and perceived needs" (2015, 38). When our strategy is driven by selfishness rather than God's purpose, it hampers our effectiveness. If your current approach isn't producing the results you desire, it's time to adopt an innovative strategy. Tomorrow's leaders tend to gravitate toward tomorrow's solutions.

As we serve in ministry, we must beware of the dangers of our "lip service." Matthew writes,

> *Not everyone who says to me, 'Lord, Lord,' will enter the kingdom of heaven, but the one who does the will of my Father who is in heaven. On that day many will say to me, 'Lord, Lord, did we not prophesy in your name, and cast out demons in your name, and do many mighty works in your name?' And then will I declare to them, 'I never knew you; depart from me, you workers of lawlessness'* (Matt 7:21–23).

This analogy of Jesus entails, the stuff you do today might be good theater, but the God who made you won't be applauding. Don't play-act for people in the ministry and then go home and neglect your family.

Authors Peter Greer and Anna Haggard, in *The Spiritual Danger of Doing Good*, warn: "Don't allow your ministry to become your mistress because you will then give the leftovers of yourself to the family" (2013, 45). As a preacher, I don't want to look in the rearview mirror and see a broken family that only received my leftovers. It's also staggering to note that 80% of preachers' spouses feel their spouses are overworked, and 50% of preachers' marriages will end in divorce. Do you think that God will be pleased that you lost your family in the pursuit of doing good? Never let your service and good works be all about you. Always give credit to God for what He has done and continues to do in your life.

Making an Impact in Today's Society

At the end of the day, week, month, year, and even your life, what will your efforts have accomplished? What kind of impact will you have made for God? The church in the book of Acts was growing because somebody was making an impact. A person's character and commitment can leave a powerful imprint on society. We are at our best when we are fully sold out for God with the mindset that I will not be defeated, discouraged, or distracted while praying fervently regarding my God given mission. Genuine leaders and committed workers are rare treasures today. A leader is first and foremost a committed Christian who has experienced a renewed mind and a pure heart. Partial commitment simply does not exist. Second, a leader is a consistent Christian, an honest person with a good reputation who always takes a stand and can be counted as reliable, steady, dependable, and unfailing.

Finally, a leader is a consecrated servant, full of the Holy Spirit and sincerely dedicated to the work of God. The duties of leadership have not changed in over two thousand years. To fulfill your ministerial responsibilities and truly make a positive impact, you must live with the end in mind. Make your ministry meaningful with a purpose. Dr. Myles Monroe once preached, "*The greatest tragedy in life is not death, but a life without purpose. You are not important because of how long you live; You are important because of how effectively you live.*" God has a plan for each of our lives. If you are living in sin, your ministry will lack meaning. If each day feels dull, joyless, or filled with dread, you are not fulfilling your purpose. Without knowing your purpose, you lack direction. The world desperately needs preachers who will teach and encourage them with the

Word of God. An old TV commercial slogan says, *"Those that mind don't matter and those that matter don't mind."* The real question every preacher should ask himself is: Am I locked into my calling, or am I clueless about it? We must always be ready to evangelize the lost and edify the saints. Our impact begins with a commitment to do the work God has called us to do.

God's Word Helps Us to Maintain Good Thoughts

To preach with conviction, one must monitor and guard his thoughts. Why is this important? If one does not control his thoughts, his thoughts will eventually control him. Our attitudes are shaped from within our inner thoughts and will influence how we feel physically and emotionally. Paul reminds us, *"Finally, brothers, whatever is true, whatever is honorable, whatever is just, whatever is pure, whatever is lovely, whatever is commendable, if there is any excellence, if there is anything worthy of praise, think about these things"* (Phil 4:8). The thoughts we entertain determine the state of our hearts and minds.

Maintaining good thoughts strengthens a man's integrity and enables him to serve God with joy and gladness. It's difficult to serve the Lord joyfully when they carry the burdens, relationship dramas, worldly desires, and other distractions that fill our souls with clutter. When our soul is cluttered, our relationship with God becomes cluttered too, affecting our spiritual well-being. We can increase your desire for God by reducing the clutter and spending more time reflecting on Him. Serving the Lord must be rooted in a God-focused mindset.

- If I'm God focused, I must have faith in a personal God. Paul writes, "So faith comes from hearing, and hearing through the word of Christ" (Rom 10:17).
- If I'm God focused, I will experience spiritual growth. A man cannot say that he is God focused and be stagnant regarding His Word. To be stagnant is to be dull and boring, but to be active and happy requires developmental growth.
- If I'm God focused, I will find my talent and share it. We serve God by serving other people. The best way to serve people is when we utilize our God given talents for His glory.

The Benefit of Sermon Preparation

Proper sermon preparation is essential for guiding your congregation in building their spiritual walk with God in the right direction. Unfortunately, many leaders go unprepared each week due to the cares and distractions of this world. To create something truly impactful, a preacher must develop a passion for the task. I've heard several preachers say they like to preach "from the overflow." That is not a problem when you have prepared and saturated his heart, soul, and mind with the Word of God. The real problem arises when you are not prepared, and the congregation senses it. It's called taking time with the Word of God. Here are some practical tips for effective sermon preparation:

- Begin your sermon prep early.
- Internalize your sermon as much as you can.

- Listen to yourself while you preach to identify areas of improvement.
- Tailor your sermon to the occasion (whether it's Founders' Day, Black History Day, doctrinal teaching, or an anniversary).
- Your personal appearance contributes to your success. There is no excuse for a slouchy appearance. Regardless of financial situation, there is no reason for soiled linen, uncombed hair, or dirty fingernails, as these can distract or turn off your listeners.
- Do not dig a grave with your fork. Attention to your health is essential to your success. Proper eating makes for spiritual gain and pulpit efficiency. Neglecting your health during the week can hinder your delivery and impact.
- Be sure to R.E.S.T. (Reflect, Engage, Surrender, and Trust). The more you get to know Jesus, the clearer it becomes that it's not about me.
- Remember, it's difficult to make a true spiritual impact on others if your flesh is stronger than your spirit.

Don't Allow One Failure to Ruin Your Ministry

People who experience failure often repeat the same actions without learning from their mistakes. Many preachers fall short because they make poor decisions without properly counting the cost. Failure to consider the consequences can lead to a lot of misery and headaches. Some ministers abandon their calling because they are swayed by what others are saying about them. Don't throw in the towel because people are talking negatively about you. After all, they talked about Jesus, too. You don't need everybody's acceptance of you, only God's. Be cautious of anyone who tells you what others are saying about you. If they truly were loyal friends, they wouldn't be comfortable letting others speak ill of you in front of them.

I've witnessed how some allow a single mistake to cause feelings of guilt and shame, leading them to condemn themselves. Consider Peter: he betrayed Jesus, but he repented and was forgiven. It is not what happens to you that truly matters; it's how you respond to it. People often fail to resolve their issues due to procrastination. There are some things in life that you should not put off for a later date, like a health concern. A doctor can detect issues early and guide you before it is too late.

A preacher once told his congregation, "I love you, but the church is not responsible for your burial. You need to get your own insurance policy and keep it current." The world is constantly changing, and we must be willing to learn. If you don't keep up in your career or ministry, you'll find yourself left behind. Just as educators and teachers attend training sessions each year to earn continuing education credits, preachers and church leaders should do the same. The purpose is to stay ahead of the education curve and continue growing. While God does not change, society, cultures, and technology do. You cannot succeed in a computer-driven world with a horse-and-buggy mindset. To reach your full potential, you must be willing to learn and adapt.

Go and Do a Good Job for God

Are we truly doing an outstanding job for Him, or are we falling short? Paul, in his letter to Titus, reminds us of our responsibilities. *"Remind them to be submissive to rulers and authorities, to be obedient, to be ready for every good work, to speak evil of no one, to avoid quarreling, to be gentle, and to show perfect courtesy toward all people"* (Titus 3:1–2). When working for God, we must always be respectful and prepared for every good work. If we are not studying or growing, we won't be ready to teach those who are in error.

I recall my high school days when the teacher would catch us off guard with pop quizzes. Without fail, someone from the back of the room would call out, "We're not ready!" The teacher would kindly respond, "That's not my fault. You should always study and be prepared for my class." The same attitude should apply in our walk with God. We must always be ready because we never know when He will choose to work through us for His glory. Expect to grow, to become stronger, and to do more for the Lord. Strive for progress in every area of your life. As you diligently serve Him, God will elevate and bless your efforts.

Thank God for your position in ministry. Paul writes to young Timothy, *"I thank him who has given me strength, Christ Jesus our Lord, because he judged me faithful, appointing me to his service"* (1 Tim 1:12). Make the most of your assignment that God has given you during your time on earth. Embrace your calling and serve with joy, knowing that God has prepared you for such a time as this.

Chapter 8
Ineffective Ministerial Training

I HAVE OBSERVED MANY YOUNG, aspiring preachers take on churches without being adequately trained. These young ministers often struggled in their ministries, and the congregation struggles as well due to the lack of a clearly communicated vision. One of my greatest rewards from working at Heritage Christian University is the opportunity to help these young ministers start fresh on a new and effective ministerial path. I recall a young preacher who once asked, "Why is my preaching so ineffective?" In Jay Adams's *Pulpit Speech,* he suggests that there are four essential arts to preaching: the art of researching content, the art of organizing, the art of language, and the art of delivery. These four acts may be simply remembered as **C.O.L.D** or **S.O.A.P**. **S.O.A.P** stands for Scripture, Occasion, Audience, and Preacher. **C.O.L.D** stands for Content, Organization, Language, and Delivery. All these elements should aim to inform, convince, and motivate (1971, 6–7).

Informative preaching requires a thorough understanding and well-researched content. Convincing preaching, also known as persuasive preaching, involves presenting facts and trusting the Holy Spirit to do the work beyond human effort. Whenever you build your ministry, start on the right foundation. Building something effective requires full commitment. You cannot succeed by doing things halfway. If you don't do ministry properly, your efforts are in vain. If we could master the basics of ministry, our lives and the impact of our work would be much more fruitful.

It's Training Time

As a Christian and man of God actively involved in ministry, we should engage in continuous training every day, whether spiritually, physically, or mentally. The more we train, the better we become. What is the importance of ministry training? Without proper training, our youth and future leaders may walk away from the church if they are not taught how to develop their faith. We have a responsibility to pass our faith to the next generation of leaders.

The most significant shaping of a child's life happens both at home and in the church. Within these environments, children develop their attitude, how they view God, and what they learn about the church and its people. They observe our criticisms, our participation in worship, and our actions as leaders. Through what we demonstrate, they determine what's truly important.

Today, we live in a time where interest in the Word of God is lessening. The greatest mistake we can make is to lack knowledge of the scriptures or God as our source. As

Jesus warns, *"But Jesus answered them, You are wrong, because you know neither the Scriptures nor the power of God"* (Matt 22:29). Failure to study and understand the Bible hampers your effectiveness and can harm others spiritually and physically. Spiritual errors can weaken the church, strip away its power, and lead believers down dead-end streets. While no one can be an expert in everything, it's great to have profound knowledge regarding scriptures.

Studying to preach can be both the best of times and the worst of times. Some days, it flows naturally; others, it's a struggle. We all love to preach, but many of us dislike the preparation that's required. Ryan Hugley, in *8 Hours or Less*, writes, "Many sermons today are filled with more pop psychology and sociological analysis than scripture" (2017, 22). In our increasingly virtual world, the audience is watching us more closely than ever. That's why we must dedicate ourselves to effective Bible study. How can professionals like doctors, lawyers, mayors, firefighters, police officers, and city council members depend on your teachings if you aren't studying well? If you feed spiritual people worldly or non-spiritual advice, they will quickly recognize that you are not making a genuine spiritual deposit into their lives.

Never begin a journey without knowing where you are headed. If you neglect your training, you'll get what you put into it. As a preacher, your tools are important. Just as a carpenter cannot build a solid foundation without the right tools, a mechanic cannot repair a car properly, or a plumber cannot fix pipes without the right equipment. Similarly, a Christian cannot be as effective without the right tools. Ministry is essential because it frees us from sin, evil, temptation, fear, depression, loneliness, resentment, and bitterness. Learn how to pray over your sermons while seeking guidance, writing out the text, and striving to understand it thoroughly.

Growing Stronger in God

The devil delights in destroying individuals, families, and especially believers. There must be a daily display of God's image in our lives. Someone is always watching what we say, what we do, and where we go. In *Guiding Your Family In A Misguided World*, Dr. Tony Evans writes, "Your behavior will tell us your personality and self-esteem. People are listening when you think they're not listening. People are watching when you think they are not watching" (1991, 48). There are ten fundamental principles that can either foster or hinder your spiritual growth in God:

1. Control your heart condition. The Word of God should govern our thought life. Joshua writes, "*This Book of the Law shall not depart from your mouth, but you shall meditate on it day and night, so that you may be careful to do according to all that is written in it. For then you will make your way prosperous, and then you will have good success*" (Josh 1:8).

2. Guard your words. Our words come from our hearts. They are either good or considered evil.

3. Cultivate a stronger prayer life. There is nothing more important in your personal life than prayer. Prayer is the lifeline between heaven and earth. Paul expresses to Timothy, "*I desire then that in every place the men should pray,*

lifting holy hands without anger or quarreling" (1 Tim 2:8).

4. Never neglect daily Bible reading. We are great at communicating with God, but we're not good listeners. The more you read, the more you will know the will of God.

5. Be a good witness for God. We are responsible for how we advertise Christ. This is done by word or conduct. Matthew writes, *"You are the salt of the earth, but if salt has lost its taste, how shall its saltiness be restored? It is no longer good for anything except to be thrown out and trampled under people's feet, You are the light of the world. A city set on a hill cannot be hidden. Nor do people light a lamp and put it under a basket, but on a stand, and it gives light to all in the house. In the same way, let your light shine before others, so that they may see your good works and give glory to your Father who is in heaven"* (Matt 5:13–16).

6. Develop a thankful heart. Thanks, from our lips alone will not reach the ears of God. To thank God is to express gratitude for the benefits received.

7. Trust God for daily needs. God knows better than we do what will be best for us. Paul writes in Philippians, *"And my God will supply every need of yours according to his riches in glory in Christ Jesus"* (Phil 4:19).

8. Prioritize love for God. You keep yourself in His love by building yourself up on the most holy faith. Jude writes, *"But you, beloved, building yourselves up in your most holy faith and praying in the Holy Spirit, keep yourselves in the love of God,*

waiting for the mercy of our Lord Jesus Christ that leads to eternal life" (Jude 20–21).

9. Remain committed to Christian fellowship. In the midst of any crisis, it's easy to forget the promises of God. Often, people are in a crisis because they have strayed away from God. In order to be successful, we must be rooted and grounded in the things of God.

10. Stay watchful and hungry for truth. One should always be prepared and ready to refuse false teaching. We have the equipment and grace to do what we need, but we often haven't developed the strength and skills necessary to succeed.

Daily Igniting Your Spirit

A good coach is always working to keep his team motivated and on fire. As preachers, we strive weekly to keep our congregations passionate for the Lord. But when you light a fire, it doesn't stay burning forever. We must daily stir up our spirit through prayer, worship, and Bible reading. Edmund Burke once said, "All that is necessary for evil to prosper is that enough men do nothing." Similarly, someone remarked, "The church with cobwebs in its collection plate is a dying church." If the church is going to fulfill its three-fold missions, it needs resources, both financial and willing individuals who are ready to serve for the greater good.

A spirit of determination will catch God's attention. Our ministry matters because people need the church. It matters because, rather than improving, the world seems to grow worse. The reason for chaos and disorder is often partial obedience, which still equates to disobedience. Disobedience stems from being disconnected from God. A question was once asked in the general church assembly: Does it really matter that I attend worship, sing, give, study, or preach? As children of God, our work truly matters. John reminds us, *"Abide in me, and I in you. As the branch cannot bear fruit by itself, unless it abides in the vine, neither can you, unless you abide in me"* (John 15:4).

Our mindset should mirror Nehemiah's willingness to roll up his sleeves because our work has eternal significance. Since we are part of the body of Christ, we each have a place, a task, and a responsibility to fulfill. Though Christ is no longer physically present, we are here to carry out His mission. If we don't preach, teach, and give, then who will? One's ministry should make an impact in the community we serve. It's our responsibility to point others to Jesus and heaven. We must teach people to put their hope in the right place. Our ministry matters because it can transform lives while helping renew their commitment to God. It teaches others how to renew their commitment to God. We must preach the Word faithfully, always be prepared, and correct the incorrect. When the church is healthy, we as believers are healthy. An unhealthy church is an ineffective church.

There are three key elements we must uphold to ensure we are a spiritually healthy church:

1. A church in tune with God is in tune with each other.
2. A church close to God will see His work in their daily lives.
3. A church aligned with God is obedient to His will.

Thank God for the church because:

- It provides "Worship" that helps you focus on God spiritually and emotionally for what lies ahead.
- ·It offers "Fellowship" that helps you to face life's problems by providing support and encouragement to other Christians.
- It facilitates "Ministry" to help fortify your faith. Remember, you cannot be aware of something of which you are not first aware!
- It deepens your "Understanding" of who Jesus is. It's not the building, the numbers, or the equipment that make a great church, but Jesus Himself.
- It offers "Salvation." The church's primary purpose is to save souls. The church must be a light for the lost, present for the sinners, loving the loveless, teaching the spiritually unlearned, and serving as a station when believers run low on spiritual fuel.

God Started A Good Work Inside of You

You are either being prepped daily for spiritual success or headed toward inevitable failure. Maintaining spiritual strength is not solely about your abilities; it's equally about your availability and your willingness to be used by God. Protection of our spiritual man requires daily diligence. You can safeguard your spirit by maintaining the right perspective, setting the right goals, and using the right strategy. There is always room for growth, improvement, and becoming better. Any work that God begins in you,

He will surely finish. We can hold onto our joy because He has started this work in us. Never let anyone tell you what you can or cannot do if God has commanded you to do it. The work He places inside of us edifies the soul and brings comfort to a hardened heart. The work within a person can transform a "bad" man into a good man. The work God deposits in us qualifies us to perform good works. For without Him, we are incapable of doing anything of lasting value. Your inner work must radiate outward. As you allow God to perform His work inside of you, it will manifest externally. Believe that God can and will accomplish it.

We Have a Job to Teach the Backsliders

Pulpit education is fundamentally about teaching, and one of the greatest dangers we face as Christians is backsliding. Church roll books are often filled with names of individuals who seldom enter the church building. When a Christian loses interest or involvement, they begin to slack in their activities, devotion, and prayer. The term backslide simply means to "turn your back on the Lord" or to "turn away from Him." Backsliding causes a person to lose spiritual passion, enthusiasm, and interest, preventing steady progress in their spiritual development. If we are not moving forward in our walk with Christ, then we are effectively moving backwards. If we aren't progressing spiritually, then we are regressing spiritually.

Backsliding is a heart issue, a sin that stems from a disregard for God's ways. Solomon states, *"The backslider in heart will be filled with the fruit of his ways, and a good man will be filled with the fruit of his ways"* (Prov 14:14). The problem arises when a person's life is governed by their own desires rather than God's. This type of person does what they want, when they want, and how they want without regard for others' opinions or feelings. It's quite possible to be sitting in the church every Sunday and still be backsliding in your heart. Remember, backsliding is not an event; it is a process. It occurs gradually over weeks, months, and even years. The prodigal son was a backslider, but he eventually came to his senses. Backsliding is similar to a tire going flat: you can put a little air in, but if the hole isn't fixed, the tire will go flat again. Most flat tires don't burst; they start with a tiny leak. You might not realize that you have a leak until it becomes difficult to steer. The same is true spiritually; you may not notice that you're going flat if the process is slow and gradual.

When God's people begin to go spiritually flat, it shows in their giving, attendance, and overall engagement. Here are some other signs that indicate a person may be backsliding:

- They spend little to no time alone with God.
- They lose their spiritual joy and enthusiasm for God.
- They have lost their passion for lost souls.
- They make it a habit of missing services on the Lord's day.
- Due to a neglected relationship with God, they invite misery into their lives.
- Their integrity and influence are hindered.
- They started out great and full of zeal, but they fell away due to not being grounded in the Word of God.

The question is: How far can a spiritually blind leader lead those who are lost? When a leader keeps his eyes on

Jesus, he will stumble less and better teach others how to walk steadily with Christ. You can't learn how to lead like Jesus unless your heart is aligned with Him. A true leader's effectiveness is rooted in the right relationship with Christ.

Chapter 9
Basic Biblical Leadership

FOR THE CHURCH TO thrive in these last days, it requires a committed "T.E.A.M." (Together Each Achieves More) that works harmoniously together. Leadership is essential to the success of any organization. Everything rises and falls on leadership. If no one is following you as you are following Jesus, then you are not truly leading. There is a vital need for godly leadership within the church. Leadership is all about taking on responsibility. It involves your time, your emotions, various relationships, and your finances. There is a difference between biblical, godly leadership and mere followership. Biblical leadership centers on reflecting the pattern of God and moving people according to His agenda. It begins with an act of faith.

Fear and faith will challenge every leader. If a leader runs away from their calling, they will find themselves bumping into it repeatedly. The New Testament sets a high standard for biblical leadership and Christlikeness. Therefore, leadership is a journey undertaken with others, as God has appointed leaders within the local church. Paul writes to the church at Ephesus,

*And he gave the apostles, the prophets, the evangelists, the shep-
herds and teachers, to equip the saints for the work of ministry,
for building up the body of Christ, until we all attain to the
unity of the faith and of the knowledge of the Son of God, to
mature manhood, to the measure of the stature of the fullness of
Christ, so that we may no longer be children, tossed to and fro by
the waves and carried about by every wind of doctrine, by
human cunning, by craftiness in deceitful schemes* (Eph 4:11–14).

Christian leaders in every generation are called to serve
and lead in every area of life. Leadership is the influence
and ability to guide others in a direction deemed important by God. Jesus was the greatest leader of all time. It's
often surprising how some individuals aspire to lead the
church but struggle to lead their families. True leadership
begins in the home by leading your own family spiritually.
As a leader, you must always be prepared, like a good
soldier for Christ. To lead properly, you must be consistent
in your walk with God through prayer and consistent
reading of His Word. You cannot give what you do not
possess. Your prayer should include asking God to help
you disciple others in a way that pleases Him.

Since God is the giver of leadership in the church, it is
the responsibility of the church leaders to recognize,
honor, and seek His divine guidance. When we evaluate
leadership based on biblical criteria, we can trust that
those leaders are called by God and appointed to serve.

A godly leader will:

- Lead the church,
- Nourish the church,
- Equip the church,
- Protect the church from unfit men, and

- Serve the church.

It is a blessing to serve in Godly leadership.

There are nine essential characteristics of a good servant:

1. Warn people of "False Teaching."
2. Be a "Faithful Student" of the Word.
3. Avoid worldliness.
4. Be disciplined.
5. Be committed to hard work.
6. Teach with authority.
7. Set an example in everything you do.
8. Builds on the scripture.
9. Grow spiritually.

We need more godly leaders as Satan's agents seek to overtake the world. Remember, godly leaders are made, not born. Many assume that leadership is inherited from family, but scripture teaches differently. Paul instructs Timothy, *"and what you have heard from me in the presence of many witnesses entrust to faithful men, who will be able to teach others also"* (2 Tim 2:2). Timothy was to seek faithful men with teachable hearts and invest in their lives so they could teach others. The greatest need in the church today is to establish sound and faithful leadership. To accomplish this, essential prayer strengthens and prepares us as we continue to work with other disciples. In the words of many older pioneer preachers, "Don't Let Your Labor Be In Vain!"

Basics of Sound Doctrine, Hermeneutics, and Homiletics

The primary goal of biblical preaching is to glorify God. Preaching, at its core, is giving the Bible a voice. To glorify God through your sermons, you must be able to rightly divide the Word of God. Sound doctrine is the foundation of a healthy life and the life of the church. It is the accurate and faithful teaching of theological truths that leads to spiritual health and transformation both individually and collectively. We should love sound doctrine because God loves sound doctrine. One might ask, "Does it really matter what we believe?" The answer is Yes, because doctrine is vital. Sadly, today, doctrine has fallen on challenging times. Many dismiss it as irrelevant, but we must remember what the Bible says about itself: it remains true and eternal.

Young preachers will benefit greatly from maintaining a good mentor, someone who can guide and encourage them in their spiritual walk with God. In *Power in the Pulpit* (1999, 73–83), authors Jerry Vines and Jim Shaddix outline four essential principles to help preachers prepare their messages:

1. The preacher must have a healthy heart and genuine motivation to guide others.
2. A healthy mind with formal education is a wonderful opportunity and a gift that God has given you. Don't neglect it. You will benefit from it.
3. A healthy body belongs to God. It is up to you to keep it intact with regular exercise, good eating habits, rest, and relaxation.

4. Maintain a healthy routine in staying disciplined in your daily Bible studies because the call to preach is also a call to prepare.

Principles of Hermeneutics

The Bible is infallible, has been accurately translated, and it is complete and final. Many self-proclaimed preachers today struggle with the Word because they have not mastered how to exegete Scripture or explain its true meaning. Life is too short to play games with the Word of God, and Scripture teaches that some need to be retaught (Heb 5:12). Therefore, it is crucial to understand the foundational principles of hermeneutics.

What is hermeneutics? Hermeneutics is the science and art of Biblical interpretation. It helps us discover and comprehend the principles that unlock the meaning of scripture's context and content. Hermeneutics is vital because it ensures we accurately understand what God is saying through His Word. It is our responsibility to interpret and apply scripture correctly. Proper interpretation is essential for proper application. If we misinterpret the Bible, we risk applying it incorrectly. Without understanding how to rightly divide the Word, we may wrongly interpret and misapply it. Jesus reminds us, "*and you will know the truth, and the truth will set you free*" (John 8:32). Our challenge is to avoid distorting the Word of God as many false prophets do today. If God has spoken, and He has, then it is profitless if we do not know what He has said. Below are common pitfalls to avoid in Bible interpretation:

- Neglecting Context: Taking a verse or passage out of its original context is a leading cause of erroneous interpretation and irrelevant application.
- Personalizing Scripture: Do not over-personalize or manipulate the text to say what you want it to say.
- Spiritualizing the Text: Do not overly spiritualize or go beyond the plain meaning of the passage. Know the content and context thoroughly.
- Injecting Your Current Thinking: Your interpretations must align with God's Word, not your personal opinions or ideas.
- Ignoring Uncomfortable Truths: Do not dismiss a scripture because it makes you uncomfortable. Always stick to the intended meaning of the text, and you won't go wrong with God.

Remember, proper hermeneutics equip us with tools to ensure our interpretations are based on the truth as God has revealed it. It helps us avoid error to the greatest degree possible, allowing us to faithfully deliver His Word.

Principles of Homiletics

As ministers of the gospel of Christ, our primary responsibility is to be the best communicators for God that we can possibly be. The biblical model for effective preaching can be seen in the life of Apollos. Paul describes him,

Now a Jew named Apollos, a native of Alexandria, came to Ephesus. He was an eloquent man, competent in the Scriptures. He had been instructed in the way of the Lord. And being fervent in spirit, he spoke and taught accurately the things concerning Jesus, though he knew only the baptism of John. He began to speak boldly in the synagogue, but when Priscilla and Aquila heard him, they took him aside and explained to him the way of God more accurately. And when he wished to cross to Achaia, the brothers encouraged him and wrote to the disciples to welcome him. When he arrived, he greatly helped those who through grace had believed, for he powerfully refuted the Jews in public, showing by the Scriptures that the Christ was Jesus (Acts 18:24–28).

Many preachers are going into the ministry for the wrong reasons. Therefore, it is crucial to understand the purpose of preaching sound doctrine. If one is going to be an effective preacher:

- He must have a message to deliver.
- He must have a purpose in delivering that message.
- He must strive to accomplish that purpose.

It's surprising how many preachers do not understand why they are preaching, who lack urgency to preach, and have no clear purpose for their ministry. The real business of a preacher is to comfort the afflicted and confront the comfortable. This underscores the importance of a solid foundation in homiletics.

What is the definition of homiletics? Homiletics is the art and science of preaching; the craft of communication that persuades, instructs, and helps listeners to truly hear what is being said. Since the Bible is alive, we must avoid making it dead or lifeless. God desires to use you in these last days; preaching is the most vital calling on earth. When done with purpose and power, your preaching can impact eternity.

Basics of Soul Winning

Soul winning is a vital calling from God, something we are to engage in daily. Our mission is to rescue people from the pits of hell. Solomon gives us wisdom in *"whoever captures souls is wise"* (Prov 11:30). God will bless you for going and bringing prospects into His kingdom. But the question remains: Are we truly giving God our absolute best when it comes to soul winning? His greatest desire is for the salvation of sinners. Every time you have the opportunity to touch someone's life, that is where you will do your best teaching and preaching. Evangelism is crucial because it yields eternal results for all lost souls. Without continual reproduction, congregations will eventually wither away. Therefore, we should all strive to do our very best in personal evangelism whenever opportunities present themselves.

From my experience as a preacher, I've observed that many people are convinced but not truly convicted of their need for the gospel. Personal evangelism is essential because many will not attend church with you, but they will listen to your personal testimony. If someone is hesitant to go to your congregation, you do not have to fall out with them. Simply share how good God has been to you. Testimony witnessing is about demonstrating God's goodness in your life, and this opens the door for relationship-building.

Do you remember the woman that Jesus met at the well? He started with her personal life, sparked her interest, and led her toward salvation. God holds us accountable for not doing His will and for failing to spark interest in the lives of those who do not know Him. He has removed our excuses for not becoming soul winners. If we neglect the Great Commission, we stand before God without excuse. You cannot win souls effectively unless you are prepared to present the message of salvation. It is vital to study your Bible and know the Scriptures well. We all need to be more involved in God's work. Soul winning is not just a calling; it's a command. Never fall into the misconception that the preacher and elders are the only ones responsible for the work. It takes a village to raise a nation. If the church is to grow, every member must show up and do their part. Each of us has a role in bringing souls to Christ; let's be about our Father's business.

Random Thoughts

- My obedience to God is more important than my image in front of others. Obedience means to "Do what He says, how He says, and all He says."
- Don't try to be everything to everybody; If you're not careful, you'll end up being nothing to nobody.
- Your history does not determine your destiny. You were created to make a meaningful contribution to society.

- Never let yourself become so busy that you neglect your relationship with God.

God's Work Is Worth Doing

There are both good and evil works taking place in this world. Each of us should regularly examine our individual work. Our work shapes us into better citizens, better servants, and better Christians. Since we are made in His image, why wouldn't we work? God has a specific plan for where we work, how we work, and what our efforts will accomplish in the lives of others. I work so that I can contribute meaningfully to society. When serving God, we must have a "Go Ye" mentality. As Jesus commands,

> *All authority in heaven and on earth has been given to me. Go therefore and make disciples of all nations, baptizing them in the name of the Father and of the Son and of the Holy Spirit, teaching them to observe all that I have commanded you. And behold, I am with you always, to the end of the age* (Matt 28:18–20).

How can we expect to be rewarded by God if we refuse to work for Him? When we take care of our divine responsibilities, God will faithfully take care of us. We must cooperate with God because He is always working. He cultivates the field, the world, the church, and each individual soul. If God is a worker and has called us to be His coworkers, then our work must be for His glory, not for ourselves. Serving God is a privilege, and His work is never finished. Sadly, it is also one of the most neglected endeavors on earth. Matthew writes, "*The harvest is plentiful, but the laborers are few; therefore, pray earnestly to the Lord of the harvest to send out laborers into his harvest*" (Matt 9:37–38). There's always a lost person nearby, needing salvation. As followers of Christ, we must establish Christlike standards for ourselves that will improve our daily walk with God. Without standards, we risk being tossed around spiritually, and our lack of discipline can hinder our service to God.

Many leaders often don't reflect on what may be hindering their service. As a leader, any obstacle that prevents you from fully serving God can also hinder others from seeing His true nature. Your worship and your works will be in vain if you lack genuine commitment.

The world remains torn between serving Christ and serving itself. You have the opportunity to give your best to God. You are in control of your life. You can choose to complain about your assignment or to complain about your circumstances, you can or you can start making a change today. Only you control your attitude, your responses, and your approach. Don't blame others because the ministry is not going the way you would like for it to go. Take ownership and pride in what God has entrusted to you. Yes, God requires your best. I want my life to matter and to leave a mark on society by doing something truly great. Make each day count with the hours that you've been given. Let your actions reflect in your relationships, your community, and your integrity in raising your children.

Learn how to show others that you appreciate your calling and that the church remains alive. Show others how to pray and walk worthy of the Lord. Paul writes to the church at Ephesus, "*I therefore, a prisoner for the Lord, urge you to walk in a manner worthy of the calling to which you have been called*" (Eph 4:1). Your walk with God depends on how well you know Him. The way you live will either honor or dishonor the Lord. As you grow in the ministry, your knowledge of God will deepen, enabling you to do His will more effectively, because Godly strength comes directly from the Word of God.

Chapter 10
Community Involvement

MANY OF TODAY'S smaller churches are declining spiritually as well as numerically. Understanding our community involves examining its demographics, cultural backgrounds, and how we can actively engage through community involvement. There are three communities we are a part of daily:

1. Our individual family community,
2. Our work community, and
3. Our church community.

Roger E. Shepherd notes several reasons why people are not actively involved in community work in his book entitled *Church Growth and Membership Involvement In A Contemporary Community* (2021, 88):

- Non-active due to UN-involvement: They make statements like we've never done this ministry here before. You don't have to wait for a church organization to do something for the community. We are the church.

- Lack of Training: Members often say that we are not equipped to do this ministry. In most cases, it is not that they aren't equipped to do this ministry; they are not willing to do this ministry.
- Exclusivism: We don't want these people in our congregation. Jesus told us to teach all men, not certain men, to be saved.
- Procrastination: Let's wait until a more convenient time. If the church is going to be relevant in the community with a growing membership, then it must be promoted by membership involvement.

People seek vibrant, healthy churches that are alive and impactful. A church that is not vibrant is often seen as forsaken. Jonathan Brooks, in *Church Forsaken*, emphasizes, "The whole mission of the church is not to convince people that they are sinners. It is to show them that life is incomplete without the unconditional love of Jesus" (2018, 133). There are no places God has forsaken, only places where the church has been abandoned. To restore the church's value, individuals must ask themselves:

- What does God want me to do, and
- Who has God created me to be?

Our mission is to strengthen the fellowship of believers and serve as a bridge connecting the community to Jesus. For the membership to grow, leaders must actively participate. Stephen Viars, in *Loving Your Community*, reminds us,

> People often do not care how much you know until they know how much you care. We want individuals in our community to constantly have reason to ask questions like, "Why did you do that for us?" or "Why did you build that for us?" or "Why did you make that available for us?" The answer to each question is simply and sincerely, because we love you! (2020, 75)

The ultimate goal of community involvement is to point the lost to the Savior. While you may not be responsible for evangelizing the entire world, the world is actively evangelizing you and keeping you in bondage through technology. Today's digital age fragments our lives, with technology acting as a powerful medium that influences us deeply. Jason Tracker, in *Following Jesus in a Digital Age*, writes,

> You are being watched and sold. Each and every day, various bits of our personal data such as searches, browsing histories, shopping habits and other data is being collected. This data is being analyzed for the purpose to anticipate our every need and allow companies to turn a profit from advertisers who are seeking our attention online (2022, 90).

Always stay focused on the will of God, and He will guide you through your life's journey.

Improving Your Spiritual Aim

The ministry is no place for a vulnerable ego. Remember, you're on a divine assignment, and God will provide everything you need. Charles B. Hodge, in his book *Getting Involved with Jesus*, stated: "Our duty to God is to serve and not rule. Man has always wished to rule. The motto suggests: Rule or Ruin, Boss or Bust. God never has wanted rulers nor glory-grabbers, but simply servants" (1970, 86-88). If we are to improve our spiritual focus, it begins with staying deeply connected to God. When our aim is off, everything else will be off. The question is: How rooted are we in the wisdom of God?

Ellen F. Davis, in her book *Getting Involved with God*, reminds us: "The early Christians knew well that even with the best intentions and the brightest hopes, we easily fall captive to the powers that destroy life. Therefore, they practiced what they called the Disciplina Arcana, the secret discipline" (2001, 180). There may be times during sermon delivery when we need to adjust the style, not the message. Style is the manner of presentation, while the message is the core substance. Although style is less important than substance, the style we choose can determine whether our message is truly heard. As you preach, always remember: God is present in the audience, as well as the people in the congregation. Your focus should be on both honoring God and communicating effectively to His people.

Releasing the Power of God in the Community

Even if you serve in a small congregation, that does not mean that your impact must be limited. Many megachurches plant smaller congregations that continue to thrive and grow. According to Shawn McMullen, in *Releasing The Power of the Smaller Church*,

> To release the power of God in the smaller church starts with the pulpit. Be careful not to preach sermons that seem to go over the heads of the audience, sermons that were so simple the hearers learned nothing new, sermons without the good news, sermons without specific applications, and sermons without biblical authority (2007, 43).

There are many effective ways to reach the community.

- Get back to the basics of faith and teach more Bible.
- Create ministries that will reach and involve the family.
- Listen for the ideas that come from outside the church rather than from within the church regarding new future ministries.

William Easum, in *How to Reach Baby Boomers*, notes,

> The primary decline of the Baby Boomers in most churches is due to their refusal to remain members when they become adults. There are two reasons as to why they are not found in the mainstream church. (1) They were never personally discipled or grounded in the faith; and (2) they were confirmed into the church rather than led to a personal relationship with Jesus Christ (1991, 74).

Authors Jill Briscoe, Laurie Katz, and Beth Seversen, in *Designing Effective Women's Ministries*, ask: "How often do we evaluate our ministry. If we have an idea for ministry, we have a God-given responsibility to see that it gets off the ground. Put feet to your idea. God gave us imaginations to further his Kingdom and to bring him glory" (1995, 44). Remember, a purpose without a process is like building a house without a plan. Every church program should aim to strengthen the fellowship among the saints and with the community. When strategy aligns with purpose, the church can truly become a powerful influence.

Positive Effects of Christian Ministry

Christian ministry is about encouraging and nurturing the growth of those seeking to deepen their understanding of Christ and His Word. As a minister of the Gospel, you should strive to be a person of value, with a well-developed mind rooted in Christ. When you develop your mind, you will discover your unique gifts and talents, enabling you to serve more effectively. There is a significant need for preachers today to address the diversity of life's challenges. Paul writes to Timothy, "*All Scripture is breathed out by God and profitable for teaching, for reproof, for correction, and for training in righteousness, that the man of God may be complete, equipped for every good work*" (2 Tim 3:16).

Many Christians seek counsel from professionals who do not incorporate Scripture into their sessions. The reason often lies in their blindness to its truthfulness and a lack of understanding. But Scripture covers every situation and remains the foundation for every human adjustment. The Word of God produces faith, cleanses our hearts, guides our decisions, imparts knowledge, and offers protection against sin. It teaches us how to "connect-up" to God and to "connect-out" to others. A man's ministry will be ineffective if he lacks a clear understanding of his role. Therefore, spiritual protection is essential, and ministerial education will prepare you to prevent burnout and sustain your effectiveness in Christ. As John C. Maxwell wisely states, "You're only as good as the people you have around you."

Marital Introduction Classes in the Community

As a local minister in our community, I have personally officiated over one thousand courthouse weddings. I began serving as a wedding officiant in 2003 at a small local wedding chapel that had strong ties with courthouses in four different cities. Usually, I would receive a call when the courthouse wedding officiant was on vacation or unable to officiate, and I would step in to fill the role. After the head wedding officiant passed away, I took the initiative to visit the courthouses, drop off my business cards, and express my desire to continue ministering in this capacity. The judges, burdened with numerous cases, appreciated the ministry opportunity that eased some of their stress and provided a spiritual blessing.

Many people seek to renew or restore their marriage, yet very few truly know how to go about it. Marriage is built through actions. Love is easy to fall into, but sustaining love over the years requires effort. After a few years of marriage, the initial excitement can fade. Phone calls become infrequent, physical contact isn't always welcome, and the small, sweet gesture that once made each other smile may now seem to irritate. Many tend to blame their spouse for their unhappiness and look outside their marriage for fulfillment. While it's possible to find temporary relief with someone else, this usually leads to even more complications, often worse situations, if the underlying issues remain unaddressed. The true key to a successful marriage isn't finding the right person; it's learning to love the person you have.

To build lasting love, it must be nurtured daily. This is called "The Labor of Love," requiring time, energy, and effort. While no two marriages are exactly alike, all couples begin with similar hopes: to have a successful, joyful, and enduring marriage. It's vital to have a vision of caring for each other as you grow older, and being committed to supporting each other through life's ups and downs.

Purpose of Marriage

Many people enter into marriage for the wrong reasons. Some marry for materialistic reasons, social status, or simply because they don't want to be alone. Others marry to escape their home environment, often settling for the first person who comes along. This approach is reckless, impulsive, and usually leads to a miserable marriage and broken family. The root of marital struggle often lies in not laying a proper foundation before tying the knot. The true purpose of marriage is :

- To provide companionship,
- To prevent sexual immorality,
- To foster an atmosphere of love, and
- To help develop each other mentally and spiritually.

Never rush into marriage for the wrong reasons. Take your time and ask yourself: "Would God be pleased with my choice?" Remember, marriage is a sacred union that should honor God and strengthen you spiritually, emotionally, and mentally.

Prepare for Marriage

Marriage is meant to last a lifetime. Preparation is essential for anything that leads to success, including marriage. Just as you prepare for a trip or a sporting event, you must prepare for the serious commitment of marriage. Jesus speaks about a man counting up the cost,

> *For which of you, desiring to build a tower, does not first sit down and count the cost, whether he has enough to complete it? Otherwise, when he has laid a foundation and is not able to finish, all who see it begin to mock him, saying, 'This man began to build and was not able to finish.' Or what king, going out to encounter another king in war, will not sit down first and deliberate whether he is able with ten thousand to meet him who comes against him with twenty thousand? And if not, while the other is yet a great way off, he sends a delegation and asks for terms of peace* (Luke 14:27–33).

One reason many marriages today are in turmoil is that too many people enter into relationships without seriously weighing the costs. The choices you make now will impact the rest of your life, and even eternity. Pray and choose wisely. A poor choice could lead to a life filled with misery. There are "Seven C's of Marriage" that should be practiced daily: Communication, Concern, Cooperation, Commitment, Courtship, Companionship, and Children. Biblical love is described

> *Love is patient and kind; love does not envy or boast; it is not arrogant or rude. It does not insist on its own way; it is not irritable or resentful; it does not rejoice at wrongdoing but rejoices with the truth. Love bears all things, believes all things, hopes all things, endures all things. Love never ends. As for prophecies, they will pass away; as for tongues, they will cease; as for knowledge, it will pass away* (1 Cor 13:4–8).

Love is a decision, an act of giving, regardless of faults, wrongdoings, or difficult circumstances. So, go ahead and love someone today.

Marriage Is a Sacrifice

Many couples struggle to manage their relationships effectively, searching for answers to their concerns. To build a healthy and lasting marriage, it's essential to understand the necessary foundation. Statistics show that married couples tend to enjoy better emotional and physical health and live longer than singles. They have the lowest rate of depression and mental disorders compared to those who are unmarried. A successful marriage requires you to focus more on your spouse's needs than your own.

If you are committed to making your marriage work, consider seriously what your spouse is asking from you (such as more help around the house, less time on the computer, TV, etc.). Remember: Anything worth having is worth working for. So, work diligently on your marriage and give God the glory. Here are some *Marriage Tune-Up Tips* that I frequently share in marriage seminars.

- Make a Commitment—Adopt a long-term perspective toward your relationship.
- Know Each Other—You should have a wealth of knowledge about your spouse: their desires, dreams, interests, and pains.
- Be Best Friends—Spend quality time doing things together. Respect and enjoy each other's company.
- Communication—Talk daily about issues that matter. Accept each other's imperfections. It's all about teamwork: the only way to solve a problem is through open and honest communication.
- Adopt God's View About Sex—Be sexually supportive and seek to give each other pleasure within the bonds of marriage.
- Remember the Good Times —Recall what attracted you to your spouse. What activities did you enjoy doing together? Continue those activities to strengthen the bond.

Marital Connections

All spouses will face differences and disagreements. The key isn't whether these conflicts happen, but how they are managed. When disagreements arise, strive to find common ground. Remember, when one spouse loses, both lose. Ask yourself: Are you willing to be the right person for your partner? Are you committed to a love that lasts, one that is fulfilling and inspiring enough for the world to want to imitate? Be intentional about establishing regular date nights to keep the love bug excited. Building satisfaction in your relationship creates happiness and contentment. This doesn't mean that you won't face problems. Instead, it signifies that you are satisfied with the person you married and committed to working through the challenges together.

- For women to feel loved: She must feel cherished and nurtured. A woman needs to recognize her value and understand that she is the most important person in her husband's world (second only to the Lord).
- For men to feel loved: He must feel honored and respected by his wife. He needs sexual intimacy, friendship (sharing activities together), and domestic support. An anonymous quote once said, "If a man's wife believes in him, he can conquer the world or at least a little corner of it."

Finally, remember the importance of connecting with others who can enrich your relationship. Building strong relationships outside your marriage can positively influence and strengthen the bonds within it.

Making a Commitment
to Making a Change

NOT EVERYONE WILL HAVE multiple opportunities in life
to create the life they desire. Every day, you will encounter
people who will appear to be suffering from emotional
pain and traumatic stress. Sometimes, you don't realize the
depth of their pain just by looking at them. Natalie
Gutierrez, in her book *The Pain We Carry*, writes: "The
pain makes sense to you, but not to everyone else" (2022,
38). When someone carries their pain day after day, it can
cause them to lose their way spiritually, especially if they
face rejection. Every man, woman, boy, and girl has experienced rejection at some point in their life. For many, these
feelings of rejection are complex and tend to lead to worry.

As ministers of the gospel, our calling is to carry the
message of salvation that helps those in pain alleviate
stress and anxiety. Jeremiah declares,

> *Blessed is the man who trusts in the Lord, whose trust is the
> Lord. He is like a tree planted by water, that sends out its roots
> by the stream, and does not fear when heat comes, for its leaves*

remain green, and is not anxious in the year of drought, for it
does not cease to bear fruit (Jer 17:7–8).

Worry is a common experience for all of us. It is simply
thoughts that suggest something bad may happen. We
don't know what the future holds, yet worry pretends to
know. It often crashes our mental party, invading our
minds with its relentless mission.

Many people in your congregation deal with worry
every week, the stress, strain, and struggle that accompany
it. Each person's relationship with worry is different; it can
affect them emotionally, physically, behaviorally, and even
their core beliefs. I often tell my congregants: You must
learn to catch and edit your worries before they catch and
edit you. Worries have a way of taking over your life if you
let them. David Carbonell, in *The Worry Trick*, emphasizes:
"In order to bounce back from your worries, you have to
reclaim your wholeness" (2016, 23). Teach those who
struggle in your congregation how to build the resilience
they need to get back up when life knocks them down.

God Is Still in the Blessing Business

God is actively seeking ministers whom He can use for
His glory. Your time spent in prayer and service for Him
does not go unnoticed. God uses those who are passionate
about Him, driven by a loving desire to serve and glorify
His name. Beginning preachers often ask, "What do I
teach those in my congregation? Every minister should
know the spiritual temperature of their congregation."
Paul reminds us, "*All Scripture is breathed out by God and
profitable for teaching, for reproof, for correction, and for training
in righteousness, that the man of God may be complete, equipped*

for every good work" (2 Tim 3:16–17). If the people sitting in the pew don't receive all Scripture, they won't have what they need to grow. Just as a doctor would tell you that a baby who doesn't receive an adequate amount milk is behind according to the growth chart, a congregation that isn't fed the Word properly will not develop spiritually.

Every church should be a praying church. I've often been asked; How do you handle being overwhelmed in life and ministry? J. Kent Edwards offers five helpful principles from his book *Deep Preaching* will help the man of God in ministry (2009, 143–150): "1) Look Backward, 2) Look Upward, 3) Look Inward, 4) Look Outward, and 5) Look Forward." In every generation, the strength or weakness of the church depends on its pulpit and teachings. When these are strong, the church becomes resilient and impactful. Preachers and teachers committed to this task make the greatest difference in the life of the church. As Steven J. Lawson states in *Called to Preach:* "A sermon is not complete until it has been applied" (2022, 156). An exposition without application is like an airplane that never lands or a piece of mail that is never delivered.

To be effective in ministry and witnessing, you must continually grow in your pulpit abilities. Your skills should never remain static. Either you are progressing or regressing. Peter encourages us, "*But grow in the grace and knowledge of our Lord and Savior Jesus Christ. To him be the glory both now and to the day of eternity. Amen*" (1 Pet 3:18). God is still in the blessing business, and through consistent growth and faithful preaching, you can participate in His ongoing work.

God's Revelation Equals Great Things

God will reveal unseen, unusual, and unsearchable things in your life that can also deliver you from your troubles. However, you will never receive the revelation you need unless you answer the call of God. Responding to that call begins with listening. James reminds us in

> *But be doers of the word, and not hearers only, deceiving your-selves. For if anyone is a hearer of the word and not a doer, he is like a man who looks intently at his natural face in a mirror. For he looks at himself and goes away and at once forgets what he was like. But the one who looks into the perfect law, the law of liberty, and perseveres, being no hearer who forgets but a doer who acts, he will be blessed in his doing."* (Jas 1:22–25).

Author Blake J. Neff, in his book *Proclamation,* identi-fies "There are four types of listening" (2007, 43–44):

1. Appreciative Listening: Listening simply for enjoyment.
2. Empathic Listening (known as Therapeutic Listening): Listening to the concerns of another in order to provide emotional support.
3. Comprehensive Listening: Listening to gain a complete understanding of one's message.
4. Critical Listening: Going beyond hearing by evaluating what you hear.

To truly receive divine revelation, we must learn to listen with our ears, body, heart, and soul. As we refine our listening skills, we open ourselves to God's great and unsearchable truths that can transform our lives and give us victory over our troubles.

Pay Attention when You Are on God's Journey

God's journey is the greatest journey I have ever embarked upon in life. Despite the obstacles and issues that arise along the way, His blessings far outweigh the challenges we may face. As you diligently serve in your ministry, be cautious of the lies and deceit of false, counterfeit, and insincere individuals. Sometimes, people lie because they do not know the truth. A single lie can cost someone their life, and worse, their soul. You can't blame others for not knowing the truth if you yourself refuse to listen to God's instructions. Search the scriptures and learn the truth for yourself. John reminds us in John, *"You search the Scriptures because you think that in them you have eternal life; and it is they that bear witness about me, yet you refuse to come to me that you may have life."* (John 5:39).

Our younger generation often lacks knowledge of our spiritual ancestors and mothers who paved the way for future generations. I thank God for those who have shaped and strengthened our spiritual walk with Him. Our preachers and teachers are the main pillars of those social settlements which we call the church. They taught us that forgiveness shows the visibility of the church. I'm thankful that we serve a God who is forgiving. Forgiveness redefines the past; it doesn't erase it, but it heals and restores. Many people struggle with forgiveness because they carry deep wounds. Jesus teaches in Matthew, *"Then Peter came up and said to him, "Lord, how often will my brother sin against me, and I forgive him? As many as seven times?" Jesus said to him, "I do not say to you seven times, but seventy-*

seven times" (Matt 18:21–22). Unforgiveness is like carrying unwanted baggage through life. To truly forgive it requires effort. Forgiveness is a four-way process for a person:

1. He must receive forgiveness from God.
2. He must confess his sins against the one he's done wrong.
3. He must receive forgiveness from the family of God.
4. He must forgive himself.

Many have resorted to suicide, substance abuse, or estranged relationships because they are burdened by unforgiveness and feel unloved. God's forgiveness is gracious and abundant. In ministry, do not let unresolved issues hinder your progress. Make things right with those you have wronged, and cultivate a forgiving spirit. How should you respond to unrepentant souls? Paul instructs us,

> *Repay no one evil for evil, but give thought to do what is honorable in the sight of all. If possible, so far as it depends on you, live peaceably with all. Beloved, never avenge yourselves, but leave it to the wrath of God, for it is written, "Vengeance is mine, I will repay, says the Lord." To the contrary, "if your enemy is hungry, feed him; if he is thirsty, give him something to drink; for by so doing you will heap burning coals on his head." Do not be overcome by evil but overcome evil with good* (Rom 12:17–21).

Jesus came from heaven's court of law to represent us and those we are called to minister to, especially the lost.

Preach the Word and remind the world of four things Jesus did for us as our Advocate.

1. He justified us: To be justified is to be declared innocent by the presiding judge.
2. He gave us an acquittal: We are released from Satan's bondage and death.
3. He exonerated our record: We were about to spend eternity in hell.
4. He redeemed us: He saved us from all of our sins. Isaiah writes, "*I am he who blots out your transgressions for my own sake, and I will not remember your sins*" (Isa 43:25).

To heal a community, honest discussions about the underlying problems are necessary. The critical question is: many are not ready to face the conversations that lead them to Jesus. He expects us to preach the Word because He is coming back. Stay on fire for God, because one day, your faithfulness will be rewarded.

Prayer!

Father God in Heaven, we humbly come before You, lifting everyone who is being called into the ministry to do Your will. We pray that You will grant them spiritual revelation and biblical wisdom as they navigate their journey wherever You send them. David's words "*Let the words of my mouth and the meditation of my heart be acceptable in your sight, O Lord, my rock and my redeemer*" (Ps 19:14). In Jesus's name, we pray. Amen!

Scripture Index

113

Bibliography

Adams, Jay E. *Pulpit Speech*. Philadelphia, PA: Presbyterian and Reformed Publishing, 1971.

Anderson, Kenton C. *Preaching With Conviction*. Grand Rapids, MI: Kregel, 2001.

Andrews, Dale P. *Practical Theology For Black Churches*. Louisville, KY: Westminster John Knox, 2002.

Briscoe, Jill, Katz-McIntyre, Laurie, and Seversen, Beth. *Designing Effective Women's Ministries*. Grand Rapids: Zondervan, 1995.

Brooks, Jonathan. *Church Forsaken*. Downers Grove, IL: Intervarsity Press, 2018.

Bryson, Harold T., and James C. Taylor. *Building Sermons to Meet People's Needs*. Nashville, TN: Broadman, 1980.

Carbonell, David A. *The Worry Trick*. Oakland, CA: New Harbinger, 2016.

Cox, James W. *A Guide to Biblical Preaching*. Nashville, TN: Abingdon, 1976.

Daane, James. *Preaching with Confidence*. Grand Rapids, MI: Eerdmans, 1980.

Davis, Ellen F. *Getting Involved with God*. Cambridge, MA: Cowley, 2001.

Davis, Reginald F. *The Black Church*. Macon, GA: Smyth and Helwys, 2010.

Dewelt, Don. *If You Want to Preach*. Grand Rapids: Baker Books, 1957.

Easum, William. *How to Reach Baby Boomers*. Effective Church Series. Nashville, TN: Abingdon, 1991.

Edwards, Kent J. *Deep Preaching*. Nashville, TN: B & H Publishing, 2009.

Engstrom, Ted W., and Ron Jenson. *The Making of a Mentor*. Waynesboro, GA: World Press Vision, 2005.

Evans, Tony. *Guiding Your Family in a Misguided World*. Pomona, CA: Focus on the Family Publisher, 1991.

Greer, Peter, and Anna Haggard. *The Spiritual Danger of Doing Good*. Grand Rapids, MI: Bethany House, 2013.

Groeschel, Craig. *#Struggles*. Grand Rapids, MI: Zondervan, 2015.

Guiterrez, Natalie. *The Pain We Carry*. Oakland, CA: New Harbinger, 2022.

Guthrie, Clifton F. *From Pew to Pulpit*. Nashville, TN: Abingdon, 2005.

Harris, James Henry. *The Word Made Plain*. Minneapolis, MN: Fortress, 2004.

Hinkle, Herbert J. *Soul Winning in Black Churches*. Grand Rapids, MI: Baker Books, 1973.

Hodge, Charles B. *Getting Involved with Jesus*. Abilene, TX: Biblical Research Press, 1970.

Holland, Thomas H. *Steps into the Pulpit*. Brentwood, TN: Penmann Press, 1988.

Hugley, Ryan. *8 Hours or Less*. Chicago, IL: Moody, 2017.

Idleman, Kyle. *Not a Fan*. Grand Rapids, MI: Zondervan, 2011.

Kinnaman, David, and Mark Matlock. *Faith for Exiles*. Grand Rapids, MI: Baker Publishing, 2019.

Larue, Cleophus J. ed. *More Power in the Pulpit*. Louisville, KY: Westminster John Knox, 2002.

Lawson, Steven J. *Called to Preach*. Grand Rapids, MI: Baker Publishing, 2002.

Lewis, Tony V. *The Message and the Messenger*. Nashua, NH: Jabez Publishing House, 2014.

Linn, Jan G. *The Art and Craft of Preaching*. Grand Rapids, MI: Baker Books, 1975.

Linn, Jan G. *22 Keys to Being a Minister*. St. Louis, MO: Chalice Press, 2003.

Low, Alvin A. *Clearing the Fog*. Henderson, NV: ACTS International Company, 2000.

MacDonald, James. *Lord, Change My Attitude*. Chicago, IL: Moody, 2001.

McKintosh, Gary L. *The 10 Key Roles of a Pastor*. Grand Rapids, MI: Baker Publishing, 2021.

McMullen, Shawn. *Releasing the Power of the Smaller Church*. Cincinnati, OH: Standard Publishing, 2007.

Mitchell, Henry H. *Black Preaching*. Nashville, TN: Abingdon, 1990.

Montoya, Alex. *Preaching with Passion*. Grand Rapids, MI: Kregel, 2000.

Morris, Derek J. *Powerful Biblical Preaching*. Silver Spring, MD: Seventh-day Adventist Ministerial Association, 2005.

Moseley, Allan. *From the Study to the Pulpit*. Bellingham, WA: Lexham, 2017.

Neff, Blake J. *Proclamation*. Eugene, OR: Wipf & Stock, 2007.

Nieuwhof, Carey. *Lasting Impact*. The reThink Group Publishers, 2015.

Paris, Peter J. *The Social Teaching of the Black Churches*. Philadelphia, PA: Fortress, 1985.

Shepherd, Roger E. *Church Growth and Membership Involvement in a*

Contemporary Community. Montgomery, AL: Amridge University Press, 2021.

Smith, Gwen. *I Want It All*. Colorado Springs, CO: David C Cook, 2016.

Thompson, Robb. *Excellence in Ministry*. Tinley Park, IL: Robb Thompson Publisher (Family Harvest Church), 2002.

Towns, Elmer T. *Winning the Winnable*. Lynchburg, VA: Church Grown Institute, 1987.

Tracker, Jason. *Following Jesus in a Digital Age*. Nashville, TN: B & H Publishing, 2022.

Viars, Stephen. *Loving Your Community*. Grand Rapids, MI: Baker Publishing, 2020.

Vines, Jerry, and Shaddix, Jim. *Power in the Pulpit*. Chicago, IL: Moody, 1999.

Wimberly, Anne E Streaty, Sandra L. Barnes, and Karma D. Johnson, *Youth Ministry in the Black Church*. Valley Forge, PA: Judson Press, 2013.

About the Author

Dewayne (Coach Tap) Tapscott is a gospel preacher with 30 years of experience, serving two congregations for over 14 years—Southwest Church of Christ in Huntsville, AL, and Piney Grove Church of Christ in Winfield, AL. He holds degrees in Business Administration from Athens State University and Theology from Heritage Christian University, along with a Master's and Doctorate in Christian Education from Christian Bible Institute & Seminary. Married to Tera, he is the father of four grown children and a grandfather. Dewayne has also worked as a teacher, varsity basketball coach, certified referee, and umpire. He serves on the Alabama State Lectureship Committee for the Churches of Christ and is an Admissions Counselor for Heritage Christian University.

Also by Cypress Publications

The Christian Life: Chapters for Bible Teachers by Ed Gallegher

Ecclesiastes: A Document Designed to Disturb by Coy Roper

Equipping the Saints: A Practical Study of Ephesians 4:11–16 by Bill Bagents and Cory Collins

Jesus the Christ: Chapters for Bible Teachers by Ed Gallagher

Silly Songs, Surprising Stories, and Supreme Court Justices: The Wild Fun-tier of Stone-Campbell Movement History by John Young

Supporting Sisters: A Biblical Approach to Helping One Another Through Life's Struggles by Kim Chalmers

WHAM! Facing Life's Heavy Hits: Thirteen New Testament Encounters by Bill Bagents and Laura S. Bagents

WHAM! Facing Life's Heavy Hits: Thirteen Old Testament Encounters by Bill Bagents and Laura S. Bagents

CYPRESS
PUBLICATIONS

An Imprint of Heritage Christian University Press

To see a full catalog of Heritage Christian University Press
and its imprint Cypress Publications, visit
www.hcu.edu/publications